Travels to and From Constantinople, in 1827 and 1828

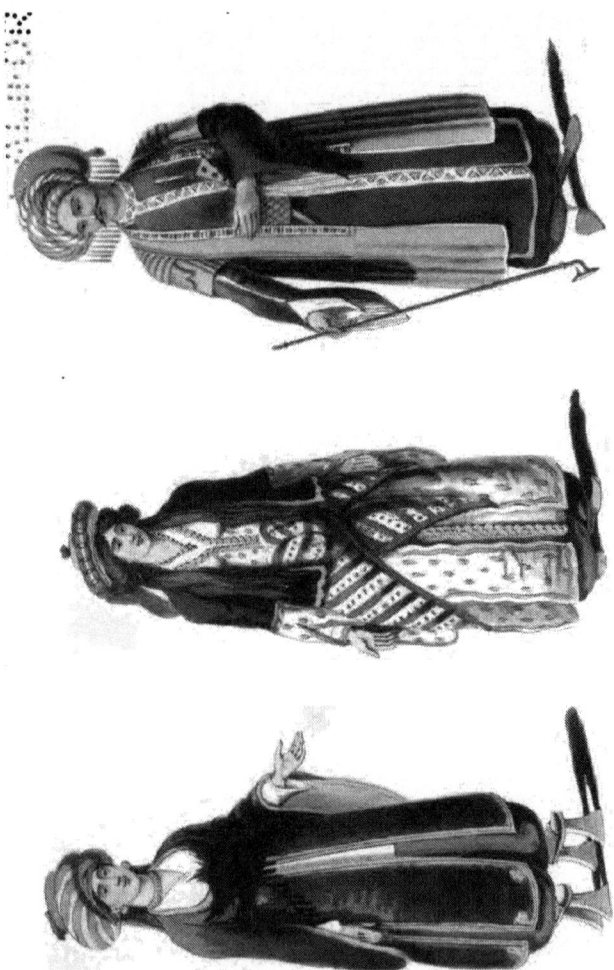

TRAVELS

TO AND FROM

CONSTANTINOPLE,

IN 1827 AND 1828.

OR

PERSONAL NARRATIVE

OF A

JOURNEY FROM VIENNA, THROUGH HUNGARY, TRANSYLVANIA, WALLACHIA, BULGARIA, AND ROUMELIA, TO CONSTANTINOPLE; AND FROM THAT CITY TO THE CAPITAL OF AUSTRIA, BY THE DARDANELLES, TENEDOS, THE PLAINS OF TROY, SMYRNA, NAPOLI DI ROMANIA, ATHENS, CYPRUS, SYRIA, ALEXANDRIA, &c.

BY

CAPT. CHARLES COLVILLE FRANKLAND,

ROYAL NAVY.

SECOND EDITION.

Illustrated with Thirty-eight Engravings.

IN TWO VOLUMES.

VOL. II.

LONDON:
HENRY COLBURN AND RICHARD BENTLEY,
NEW BURLINGTON STREET.
1830.

DR 42?
F 8
v. 2

GIFT OF
PROFESSOR C. A. KOFOID

CONTENTS

OF THE SECOND VOLUME.

CHAPTER I.

Ride to Solima.—Aqueduct.—Druse Castle at Brumana. —View of Mar Mousa. — Village and Palace of Solima. —Capuchins. — Evening Scenery. — " Debs."— Christian Emir.—French Doctor.—Custom of blessing the Silkworm's eggs.—Druse and Christian Arabs.—Tantoura.—Terror of Children at the sight of my white turban and dog Ponto. — Departure for Buckfaya. — Sick people near Thannes.— View from the summit of a mountain.—Buckfaya.—Costumes.—Cheating disposition of Arab Muleteers.—Departure from Buckfaya.—Description of the Country.—Sarcophagus near Ahtouta.—Bivouack at Ahtouta, and Supper with Arab Sheiks.—Promise of hidden treasures.—Ponto's vigilance.— Search for treasure; disappointment of Sheiks.—Departure from Ahtouta.—Facra with its ruined Temples.—Tombs.— Remarkable rocks.—Nahr el Leben and natural Bridge.— Bivouack upon Gebbail Sennin.—Naitra.—Akoura.—Metooali and Bedouins.—Plains on the Upper Region of Lebanon.—Bivouack near Old Harrissa.—Cedars of Lebanon. —Bsherri.—Carmelite Convent.—Departure for Ainette.— Conduct of my guide.—Parley with Arabs.—Deir el Akmar. —Mr. Bird.   -   -   -   -   -   - 1—60

CHAPTER II.

Departure from Deir el Akmar.—Remarkable excavation. —Corinthian column.—Baalbeck.—Description of the ruins. —River Djoush.—Visit from the Emir's people.—Conduct of Jiaccomo.—Behaviour of Muleteer.—Reference to Cogia Bashi.—Magisterial proceedings.—New arrangements.—Curiosity of the populace, and political conversation.—Fresh embarrassments.—Fracas among the natives.—Good conduct of Greek curate.—Departure from Baalbeck.—Zurgaia.— Bivouack.—Zerbdeni.—Souk, and antiquities.— Dumar.— View of Damascus. — Entrance into the city.—Capuchin convent.—Terra Santa.—M. Bodin.—Description of Damascus.—Lazarites.—Plague.—Departure from Damascus. —Dimass.—Apprehensions of ambuscade.—Khan el Margi. —Ascent of Mount Lebanon.—Druses.—Khan el Lassan and bivouack. — Descent towards Bairout. — Arrival at Bairout.   -   -   -   .   - 61—128

CHAPTER III.

Strangways sets off for Cairo. — A Greek squadron comes into the port of Bairout.—I set off for Jerusalem.— Khan Bourghaldi.—Tombs.—Djissir Damoor.—Ancient remains.—Nabyoonas, the place of Jonah's miraculous disembarkation.—View of Saide.—Khan el Aoule.—Visit to Lady Hester Stanhope at Djouni.—Saide, or Sidon.—Intelligence of the Battle of Navarino reaches us.—Embarrassments.— Generous offer of protection from a Metooali Chief.—I abandon my projected journey to Jerusalem for the present.— Anecdote of Sultan Mahmoud and Mehmet Ali Pasha.—I leave Djouni for the Palace of the Emir Beshir (Prince of the Druses).—Reception from the Emir.—M. Aubin's account of Navarino, and advice how to proceed.—Plague at Deir el Kamaār.—Abdha.—Arrival at Shia, near Bairout.—Maronite curate, his daughter, and hospitality.—Arrival at Mansouree. —I go to Deir el Kalaā.—I am attacked by the fever of the country.—Return to the neighbourhood of Bairout.—Projects for departure to Alexandria. — His Majesty's ship Pelorus arrives.—I embark in her for Cyprus and Alexandria. —Miscellaneous remarks on Syria. - 129—189

CHAPTER IV.

Departure for, and arrival at, Alexandria.—I am obliged to abandon my project of ascending the Nile.—Arrival of the *débris* of the Turco-Egyptian fleet from Navarino.—Visit to the Antiquities of Alexandria.—We sail with convoy for Malta. — Arrival at Malta. — Quarantine. — La Valetta.— Carnival gaieties. — Opera. — Presentation of the Flag of Saint George.—Preparations for departure for Sicily and Italy -   -   -   -   -   -   190—214

CHAPTER V.

Etna, Taormina and Messina.—Stromboli.—Capri and Vesuvius.—Arrival at Naples.—Visit to Pompeia.—Recent discoveries.—Studio.—Vases, bronzes, &c. &c.—Departure for Rome.—Appearance of the country.—Doganieri.—Arrival at Rome.—Recent improvements.—Antiquities, &c. &c.—Studios of Sculptors.—Departure from Rome.—Nepi and Civita Castellana.—Loss of Ponto.—Terni.—Foligno.—Nostra Signora D. A.—Perugia.—Lake of Thrasimene. — Ramaggio. — Florence. —Gallery. — Palazzo Pitti. — Cascine, &c. &c.— I recover Ponto.— His adventures   -   -   -   -   -   215—265

CONTENTS.

CHAPTER VI.

Departure for and arrival at Bologna.—I am attacked by the fever, while at the Gallery of Pictures.—Ferrara, Padua.—Banks of the Brenta.—Fusina.—Venice.—Piazza San Marco.—Ducal Palace.—Bridge of Sighs.—Pozzi.—Church of Saint Marc.—Arsenal.—Marchese Paulucci.—Kremnitz copper.—Reflections on the state of Venice.—Churches.—Pictures.—Canova's tomb, &c. &c.—Promenade *en bateau* to the Lido.—Departure for Trieste by steam-packet.—Trieste.—Adelsberg; its grotto of stalactites.—Conduct of innkeeper and postmaster. — Laybach. — Franz. — Mahrbourg.—Gratz.—The Semmering.—Neukirchen.—Arrival at Vienna.—Conclusion. - - - - 266—301

ERRATA.

VOL. II.

Page 97, line 8, *for* 'Muckrown,' *read* 'Muckrow.'
 — 135, — 29, *for* 'are,' *read* 'here.'
 — 215, — 9, *for* 'Cetti,' *read* 'Pitti.'
 — 229, — 21, *for* 'Warren Hastings, Anderson.' *read* 'Warren Hastings Anderson.'
 — 235, — 6, *for* 'sacs de nuits,' *read* 'sacs de nuit.'
 — 230, — 21, *for* 'Torwalsen,' *read* 'Thorwalsden.'
 — 277, — 9, *for* 'Laguni,' *read* 'Lagune.'

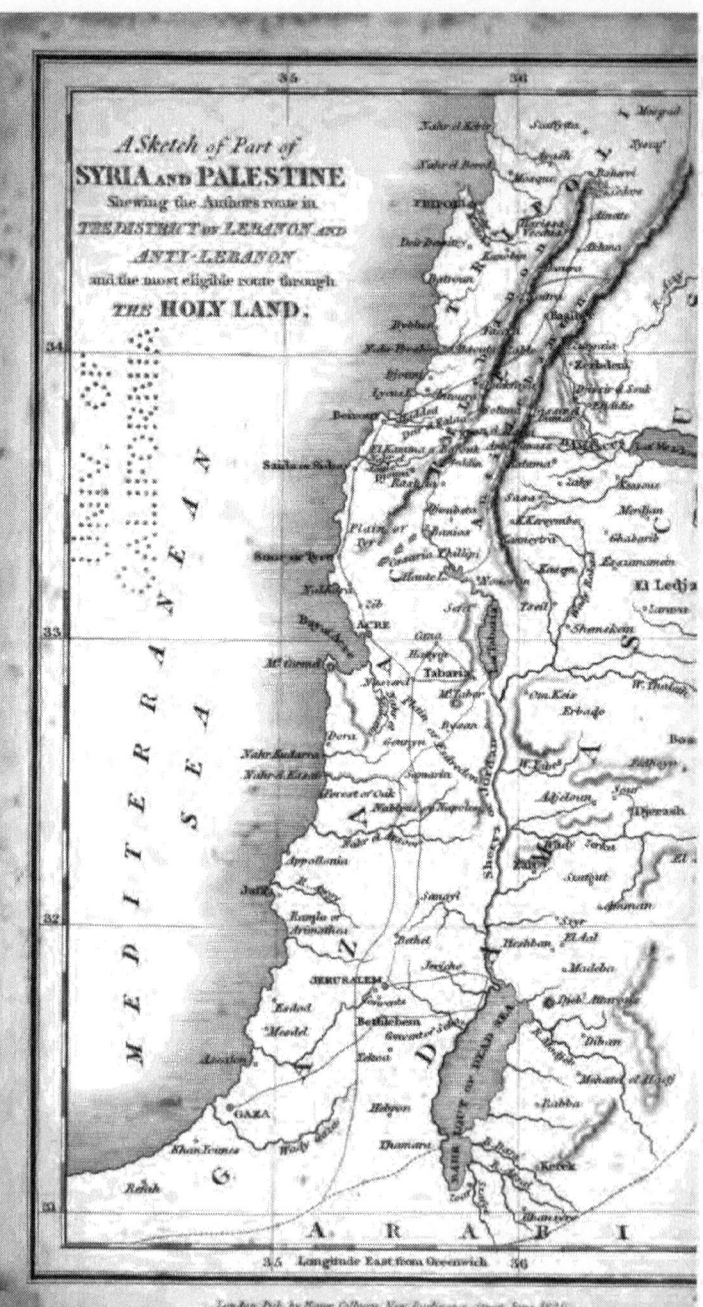

JOURNAL OF A TOUR

IN

MOUNT LEBANON, THE BACKAA-METOO-ALIS, AND ANTI-LEBANON.

CHAPTER I.

Ride to Solima.—Aqueduct.—Druse Castle at Brûmana.—View of Mar Mousa.—Village and Palace of Solima.—Capuchins. — Evening Scenery. — " Debs."— Christian Emir.—French Doctor.—Custom of blessing the Silkworm's eggs.—Druse and Christian Arabs.—Tantoura.—Terror of Children at the sight of my white turban, and dog Ponto. — Departure for Buckfaya. — Sick people near Thannes.—View from the summit of a mountain.—Buckfaya. — Costumes. — Cheating disposition of Arab Muleteers.—Departure from Buckfaya.—Description of the Country.—Sarcophagus near Ahtouta.—Bivouack at Ahtouta, and Supper with Arab Sheiks.—Promise of hidden treasures.—Ponto's vigilance.— Search for treasure: disappointment of Sheiks.—Departure from Ahtouta.—Facra, with its ruined Temples.—Tombs.—Remarkable rocks.—

Nahr el Leben and natural Bridge.—Bivouack upon G
bail Sennin.—Naitra.—Akoura.—Metooali and Bedoui
—Plains on the Upper Region of Lebanon.—Bivou[
near Old Harrissa.—Cedars of Lebanon.—Bsherri.—C
melite Convent.—Departure for Ainette.—Conduct of
guide.—Parley with Arabs.—Deir el Akmar.—Mr. Bird

OCTOBER 1, 1827.—This morning I stru[
my tent, under which I had passed about
month in one of the most beautiful positions
the world, and set off after breakfast with M
Maddox, for Solima, an Arab town in the hea
of the mountains, about four horse hours fro
Der el Kalaā. We were mounted upon asse
and followed by our servants with a long trai
of baggage, most of which, I blessed my star
belonged to my companion.* Our way led ov[

* My travelling equipment consisted of a Mameluke dres
an European cloak, with which to cover myself in rain an
at night; two small Turkey carpets, which served for sea
table, and bed; a small Russian valise which I had purchase
at Bucharest, which contained my wardrobe, and did duty [
pillow for my head; and a pair of small Turkish saddle-bag
made at Cyprus, which held my dollars and ammunition, m
washing and toilette apparatus, my portfolio, with a spar
shirt and cap, and sometimes a bottle of wine or arrack, a
the case might be. My arms were, a Turkish sabre, a brac[
of pistols, and a double-barrelled gun. My servant Yacoul
carried a large pair of saddle-bags, (hordjee,) in which wer[

the crest of the mountains to the northward, passing through the village of "Betmerri" and "Ail Berdi."

At about noon we came to the commencement of the ruined aqueduct of Berytus.* The water came originally from Mar Mousa, a convent on the top of a high mountain, about an hour farther on. In this part of the aqueduct there are no arches, but merely a solid stone channel, most part of which is still very perfect, raised about five or six feet from the level of the ground. These ruins are on the left hand, close to the road.

packed the culinary utensils, consisting of a large tin pot, in which to make soup or pillau, a coffee pot, two cannisters, the one containing ground coffee, and the other pounded sugar, three finjans or coffee cups, a drinking cup of gilt brass, and a leather pouch for salt and pepper. This small stock completed my list of necessaries, and of a truth I needed nothing more. Yacoub likewise carried his clothing in this same invaluable pair of saddle-bags, and stowed away in them bread, cheese, onions, flesh, cold meat, figs, grapes, raisins, walnuts, &c. &c. He was armed with a long musket and a sabre, and the Sieyes, or Muckrow, had likewise his gun, and a handjar in his girdle. These men carried likewise their pipes and pouches of tobacco; but as I was no smoker, I did not encumber myself with these articles.

We now passed over some extremely rugg[ed]
and dangerous ground, and close to the to[wn]
of some Sheik; and arriving at the village [of]
Brumana, were delighted to find there, in [an]
elevated position, a fine handsome castella[ted]
palace, the residence of four Druse princes, [or]
emirs, with their families. There is a garden [in]
front, and a most luxuriant and tempting vi[ne]
yard, the fruit of which hung in luscious clust[ers]
over our heads; but not with impunity, as [we]
ate abundantly of the refreshing bunches.

At about two o'clock we began to descend [a]
most precipitous road towards the bed of t[he]
river Berytus, which was now almost entire[ly]
dry. The scenery all around was extreme[ly]
savage and grand, more particularly at o[ne]
point, when upon suddenly turning round t[he]
angle of a projecting rock, the eye was co[n]
ducted up a tremendous succession of precipice[s]
surmounted by the convent of Mar Mousa[*]
towering aloft in the sky :—I should have sai[d]
convents of Mar Mousa, there being one o[f]

---

* Mar Mousa signifies in Arabic, "Saint Moses."

the Maronite catholic and one of the Greek communion in this place.

The bed of the river abounds with olianders, (*laurea rosa*) which by contrasting the blushing pink of their blossoms and the glossy green of their long leaves, with the huge grey rocks and pebbles of the now dried up channel, produced a beautiful effect. Upon this bottom stands a little water-mill, belonging to the Capuchin convent of Solima, which contrives, by means of a little dam, to economize sufficient water, even at this season of drought, to turn its lazy wheel; but in so doing, deprives the bed of the river of almost all its aliment.

After stumbling through the rocks which encumbered our path, we began to ascend one of the steepest zig-zags on the opposite mountain which I have ever seen; and after a tedious half-hour, during which we were obliged occasionally to halt the baggage-asses for rest, reached a very large and handsome palace, the residence of the Emir [*] of Solima, a Christian Arab. This edifice is likewise cas-

[*] Hyder Emir.

tellated, and would not disgrace a more civili[s]
prince or country.

Passing through the dirty village of Soli[ma]
we arrived at the Capuchin convent at ab[out]
4. 30. and were kindly received by Pa[dre]
Niccola, (Napolitano,) who embraced my c[om]
panion and hugged him in his arms w[ith]
the greatest joy, he having been here tw[ice]
before. I must own that I did not much en[joy]
so close a contact with the greasy garb of [the]
worthy Capuchin. Here we were tolera[bly]
lodged in separate apartments, where we fou[nd]
good beds, a luxury I had been for some ti[me]
unacquainted with. We dined with the wort[hy]
monks at sunset, our other host being Pa[dre]
Modesto,* (Romano,) of venerable but seduct[ive]

---

* Padre Modesto, among the many interesting anecd[otes]
which he related to me, mentioned the following circumsta[nce]
of which he was himself an eye-witness.

When Napoleon had caused himself to be acknowled[ged]
by the Porte as Sovereign of France, he sent orders to all
French consuls in the Levant, to find out, by proclamati[on]
all such persons as could, by proving their descent fro[m]
French stock, claim the protection of the Consular fla[g of]
that nation.

At Smyrna, where Padre Modesto was at this pe[riod]

appearance, and suave manners. Our conversation turned principally upon the manners and customs of the Druses, Maronites, Ansari, and other inhabitants of the extensive dominion of the Emir Beshir, and likewise upon the success of the Protestant missions among this people.

These monks are both liberal and (for Capuchins) enlightened men; they have in their possession some of the Bibles in Arabic and Italian, which are distributed by the missionary societies; and they say that the only objection made by the bishops to their further distribution is,

residing, many persons came forward and proved themselves to be the descendants of the Crusaders of the Lily; among the rest, a very interesting young girl, who kept a kind of shop where she sold things upon commission, (Sensale,) appeared at the chancery of the Consulate, and producing several original documents, clearly established her claim to be considered as the sole surviving representative of the House of Lusignan!

The Consul made a report of this extraordinary fact to his Government, who ordered him to inquire into the circumstances of this humble but interesting scion of a royal line, and to provide handsomely for her future existence. If my memory serves me truly, I think Padre Modesto added, that he heard many years afterwards that she had married a Christian merchant of Cyprus, and that she died without issue, at Larneca, or Famagousta, in that island.

that *they do not contain the Apocryphal boo[k]*
This is a curious fact, and I leave it to t[he]
reader to draw his own inferences from it.

Our dinner-room, like that of most of t[he]
principal houses in the mountains, was open [to]
the air in the front, which is supported by tw[o]
arcades, and looks down through a pretty litt[le]
garden, full of pomegranates and myrtles an[d]
vines, into the deep dells of the valley, throug[h]
which the river Berytus winds its now laz[y]
course, but which, when swelled by winte[r]
rains, must form a tremendous cataract.

As the evening advanced, the moon arose i[n]
all the splendour of these mountain climates, an[d]
shed her silvery beams over a scene calculated t[o]
excite the most bewitching but impressive sen[-]
sations: the breeze was loaded with the perfume[s]
of the most aromatic shrubs and flowers, the star[s]
shone like burning emeralds in their cloudles[s]
vault; all nature breathed in silence and repose[,]
save the watchful house-dog of the Arab, wh[o]
at fitful intervals bayed at the lovely moon, o[r]
warned by his threatening bark the sly and

furtive jackal, which ever and anon gave notice of his approach by his shrill and plaintive cry, which so much resembles the wailing of an infant, as to startle the unaccustomed ear of the traveller, and drive a pang into his heart. Such was my first evening at Solima.

October 2.—I arose, after a calm and refreshing sleep upon the good monk's bed, but found the contrast between it and the carpets upon which I had for some time reposed, rather unfavourable to the latter (a traveller in the East had better not expose himself to it, lest he should regret such luxuries).

After breakfast we walked about with the Padre Niccola, and saw the process of making "*debs*," a saccharine substance extracted from grapes, and used by the mountaineers as a substitute for sugar. It is in process somewhat similar to wine-making, with the exception of being boiled and cooled alternately twice. The grapes are trodden out upon a kind of stone platform, a white earth like gypsum being thrown upon them from time to time, to make them bind together: the

juice, running off the platform, through a li
channel, is received in a basin cut in the r
from whence it is carried in buckets to
boiler, from the boiler to a second basin, wl
it is skimmed and allowed to cool; it is bo
and cooled twice, and then put into g
earthen jars, and becomes a rich syrup.

The position of this "debs" manufactory
indeed lovely: it stands on the side of the mo
tain, beneath a forest of pines, and amidst
most luxuriant vineyards and mulberry garde
which, throughout the mountains, form
many successions of parallel terraces. The Ar
being well aware of the necessity of protecti
their superficial soil against the descent of
winter torrents, construct walls, like flights
steps, and thus banking up, and accumulati
the earth, render the sides even of natura
barren rocks teeming with fruits and verdi
and flowers.

What a pity that such lovely spots should
visited and laid waste by the pestilence! T
plague is in many villages all around us, t
the Emir has the good sense to plant guardi

CASTLE AND VILLAGE OF SOLIMA.

at all the intersecting roads in the immediate neighbourhood, and thus cuts off communication with the infected places. He is, as well as all his family, in strict quarantine.

October 3.—The weather most delightful and temperate. I walked about, accompanied by my faithful Ponto, enjoying extremely the beauty of the country, and made a rough sketch of the Emir's palace, the convent, and the flat-roofed village embosomed in vines. The woods all around me abounded with myrtles, arbutus, gum sistus, wild-sage, thyme, laurea rosa, wild vines, and Valonia oak. The botanist might have discerned abundant treasure among the sylvan plants and flowers, which sprang up luxuriantly on every side; and the geologist would have found quantities of iron, the oxyde of which reddens the rocks and rich earth all around. This mineral, indeed, abounds in the mountain, and, as I learn, so does coal, and in some places gold.

Upon my return to the convent, I found there, sitting upon the ground, in a corner of the yard, surrounded by his dependents, a Christian emir of the neighbourhood, who had come down to the chapel of the convent, to pray and purify. He was in quarantine, and did not suffer us to approach very near to him. He was a rude but good natured person, and a good specimen of the native princes of Lebanon.

After dinner, I was much edified by a long conversation with Padre Niccola, respecting the death of a young Druse princess, whose friend and confident he was. His description of the struggle in her mind for mastery between paganism and Christianity, was most affecting and curious. He had even obtained possession of the *sacred book* of the Druses,—for he was her executor,—but he refrained from perusing *the impious pages*, from motives to him highly creditable, although in a worldly point of view blameable. His conscientiousness induced him to restore to her parents that deposit of all the mysteries of the Druse religion, which has so long and so earnestly been sought for by the curious of the Western world.

OCTOBER 4.—A Frank doctor, a native of

Picardy, who has dwelt twenty years in the mountains, arrived this morning from Buckfaya, to confess and purify. I was much pleased by listening to his conversation with the good monks, respecting the wars of the mountains, and the customs and prejudices of the various tribes who inhabit this interesting region.

October 5.—The doctor returned to his village; the weather was rather hotter, but did not prevent me from rambling over the hills and dales with old Ponto, in search of fine scenery, which indeed abounds in all directions.

On returning I entered the neat little chapel of the convent, and here I found suspended from the roof, upon curiously shaped bags of paper, quantities of silk-worms' eggs, which are left here by the Christian Arabs to be blessed by the priest at particular seasons of the year. Silk is the staple commodity of the mountain, and is exported from Bairout to Marseilles and Barbary.

In my walks I sometimes enter the houses both of Druse and Christian, and find them generally clean and comfortable; the women with their tantoura* and veil, are decent and comely in their manners, although beauty seems to be rare among them.

The children generally ran squalling and screaming away, terrified by my Turkish garb,

* The custom of wearing the horn, or tantoura, may be traced to a very remote antiquity.

The lifting up of horns is a common figure of speech in the Scriptures.

" Lift up not your horn on high, speak not with a stiff neck."—Psalm lxxv. v. 5.

" All the horns of the wicked also will I cut off, but the horns of the righteous shall be exalted."—Psalm lxxv. v. 10.

In Abyssinia the men wear two horns, or tantouras; and I have heard that upon some coin commemorative of Alexander the Great's visit either to the High Priest of Jerusalem, or the High Priest of Jupiter Ammon in the Libyan desert, the Macedonian king is represented as wearing one or two horns.

He was commonly styled in the figurative language of prophecy, " him of the two horns :" whereby some commentators suppose to be meant the horns of the Crescent, and others the horns of the Eastern and Western world, but which probably have reference to the circumstance of his wearing two horns or tantouras.

The statue of Moses, by Michael Angelo, upon the Quirinal Hill at Rome, represents the prophet as wearing two horns.

I venture to throw out these hints, with all humility, to the consideration of antiquaries.

white turban, and dog, which latter the Arabs generally took for some strange and fearful animal, they having never before seen an English pointer, which indeed is a very distinct-looking creature from the mongrel curs which infest the East. Three luckless urchins, loaded with firewood, were so terrified by my suddenly appearing before them in the forest, that they threw down their loads and ran screeching and yelling down a precipitous descent, never once venturing to look behind them, and paying no attention to my conciliatory gestures and exclamations.

It is no wonder that the Rayas of the Porte should not dare to face their masters in the field, when such is the terror of the Turk implanted in the bosom of the Arab, Greek, and Armenian infant. The earliest impressions are generally the most durable, and the tales of the nurse become insensibly intertwined with our maturer imagination, till they at last assume the appearance of reality.

I was accompanied in my day's ramble by a

very interesting child, the son of a French merchant at Bairout, who had been sent here by his parents to learn Arabic, under the guidance of Padre Modesto. His tender age and innocent prattle interested me very much.

Mr. Maddox talks of remaining here, but I must be moving on towards the Cedars, Baalbeck, and Damascus, ere the season becomes unfit for travelling.

OCTOBER 6.—After breakfast, at ten o'clock, I took leave of my companion Mr. Maddox, and the good capuchins, and set off with two asses and Ponto, for Buckfaya. We descended on foot a precipitous and rough road for about three quarters of an hour, when we crossed the bed of the river Berytus, and began to ascend the opposite mountain, over a most execrable and almost perpendicular road, much worse than any of the *Ladreras* in the Andes, which I went over eight years ago. On my left hand, about half-way up the mountain, I was shown a church constructed, as far as I could learn, by the primitive Christians. It is a huge cavern excavated in the rock, but has a wall of hewn stone facing the valley. It contains about forty different apartments; but the heat of the day was so excessive, and the access to this curiosity so difficult, that I did not visit it. I ascended on foot the road over this mountain, for about three hours, suffering extremely from the heat, which in these deep rocky valleys is accumulated to a surprising degree; reposing twice under shady trees covered with grapes, by the side of fountains, one of which (that nearest Solima) is very beautiful.

Here I was surrounded by sick people, who hearing of the arrival of a Frank traveller, came to him to be healed. It was in vain that I assured these poor people that I was no hakim (physician); they paid no attention whatever to my disclaiming all pretensions to the healing art; and I was compelled to prescribe such simple medicines and treatment as appeared to me unlikely to do the poor sufferers any harm. Among the most clamorous and exigent of my patients was a very pretty young woman, whose complaint seemed to be chiefly the being plagued with an old sexagenarian husband. For her, I could only prescribe a cooling diet and a plentiful dose of patience. Near this first fountain, to the left, is the village of "Thannes," where there was the plague.

At about 12. 30. I reached the village of "Douar," where I reposed for an hour, feasting upon the fine luscious grapes which hung invitingly around me.

When I reached the top of the mountain, a splendid view burst upon me; Deir el Kalaä with its forests of pines, on my extreme left; the sea, with Bairout, its plains covered with verdure, and its bright red sands, in my front; on my right, the mountains of "Buckfaya," clothed with forests and studded with convents, Greek, Maronite, and Armenian; and on my rear, the valley of Berytus, with the towers of Solima rising above it. As I approached Buckfaya, I met some very fine droves of mules and asses, from Baalbeck and Zahle and Damascus. I reached Buckfaya at 2. 30. very much tired and heated, my head aching tremendously, and my pulse threatening an attack of fever. My poor companion, Ponto, suffered extremely from the heat, and could scarcely drag himself along. I alighted at the house of a respectable-looking Arab, who gave me a large open verandah to repose in, from whence I had a fine view of the highest hills in Mount Lebanon, the sea on my left, and the town of "Buskinta" on my right.

To-morrow I propose going on towards my northernmost point, the Cedars, which I hope to reach on the second day. I spent the whole evening in my verandah, reposing in the cooling breeze, and enjoying the beautiful prospect which lay before me. At nightfall I invited mine host and the village schoolmaster to take coffee with me, my servant Jiaccomo performing the part of dragoman. The schoolmaster had, alas! lost his school. He had been established in this important post by the American missionaries; but the hand of power interposed, and scattered his flock like the sand of the desert. The Maronite patriarch well foreseeing the consequence of education, crushed, by his anathemas, this germ of civilization, and thus destroyed the only hopes which *rational Protestants* can entertain of dispelling the Cimmerian darkness which overshadows the minds of these benighted people.

During the night I was devoured by fleas, and could get no rest until daylight released me from the incessant attacks of this light infantry; but the beauty of the nearly full moon which shone in upon me, while it lighted up the grand features of mountain scenery, compensated me for the absence of sleep.

Sunday, October 7.—The weather beautiful, but excessively hot. I took a long morning ramble, and was much amused with the costumes of the Maronite women, as they went to church in full dress. The most remarkable feature in this costume is the tantoora, perhaps the most singular head-dress in the world. This is a long silver or wooden horn, about twelve or fourteen inches in length, shaped something like a speaking trumpet, and projecting from the forehead in an upward direction. Over this unicorn-looking instrument, the veil (of white muslin, or calico if Christian, and black if Druse) is thrown, which closing across the face, at the will of the wearer, and falling down the shoulders behind, has not altogether an ungraceful appearance. The wives and daughters of the Emirs and great Sheiks have the tantoora richly gilt, and in some instances embossed. The rest of the costume consists of a feridgee, or large gown, a pair of trowsers, and slippers. The hair of these ladies is plaited down the back in long separate braids, to the end of each of which is attached a kind of ornamented silver weight. For a more perfect description of this costume, I must refer to my sketch book; a few strokes of the pencil conveying images more accurately to the mind, than the most laboured expression of the pen.

On returning home, I found that I had failed in my attempt to procure mules for this day, the Arabs choosing to repose, and go to church,

in preference to broiling along the mount
in the sun. It was impossible to question
propriety of their motives [e cosi pazienza.]

October 7.—I walked out again in
course of the evening, but found it too hot
be agreeable. In the evening I enjoyed a m
delicious solitary ramble upon the side of
mountain towards "Mars Elias," an Armen
convent, where the Bible and other holy bo
are printed in Arabic. My path led unde
forest of pines, full of myrtle, arbutus, and
niper; the sea was on my left, far down bel
me; and the sun went down in such a blaze
glory as is difficult to be conceived.

On my return home through the lower part
the town of Buckfaya, I had some difficulty
saving poor Ponto from lapidation, and w
obliged, in his defence, to collar an Arab, a
hold a pistol to his breast, ere he would des
from pelting my old friend and companion.
have often been much amused by the fear whi
the appearance of an European dog excites
the Turks and Arabs; but upon this occasio

my nerves were excited by other than risible feelings. At night, besides the usual annoyance of fleas, I was kept awake by mine host's sons, fine handsome young fellows, who amused themselves until a very late hour, by singing songs and *improviséing* amatory poems, in all the monotony of Arabic recitative, which, of all the music I have ever heard, is the most tedious and painful to the ear.

October 8.—The early part of this morning was spent in successfully resisting the attempted impositions of the various muleteers who came to offer their services. I at last concluded a bargain for two fine mules and an ass, for five days' journey, for one hundred piastres, the muleteer having begun by insisting upon receiving three hundred beforehand. These five days, I calculated, would carry me to Baalbeck, at which place I reserved to myself the right either of taking the same animals on to Damascus, or providing myself with others. I was prevailed upon by my servant to pay the one hundred piastres in advance, an arrangement

which I had afterwards, as will be shown, 1
son to repent of; indeed, the muleteer wo1
not stir until the money was deposited in
hands of his mother; I taking care, upon 1
part, to call in mine host and the schoolmas1
as witnesses of the transaction. I set off
nine o'clock for the ruined temples of Fac
upon the highest ridge of the mountain.

I passed again the convent of Mar Elias a1
through the forest, and soon began to ascend
volcanic-looking mountain, the stone of whi(
seemed to have gone through the process
fusion, and was full of *smaller stones* and *circul(*
black specks. After reaching the summit (
this mountain, I began to descend towards th
source of the Dog's river (Nahr el Kelb): th
water ran into a deep rocky basin, and looke
as green and as clear as an aqua marin(
Ponto, as if aware of the propriety of the ac
tion, bathed in the green flood.

I now ascended a hill of (what appeared t(
me to be) pummice and lava, reaching a littl(
village called "Bomeson," at eleven. Here w(

reposed for a few minutes under a fine Valonia oak, and then descended into a kind of inverted cone, (query, the crater) for half an hour; crossed Nahr el Kelb again, and ascended a terrific road over blocks of lava and grey limestone, reposing twice under natural bowers of vines, the heat being excessive. We reached the top of the mountain at fifteen minutes past one, and from thence had a fine but very distant view of Bairout and the shipping.

We dined upon cold provisions, (with which we had stored our saddle-bags at Buckfaya,) under a lovely little arbour of Valonia oaks and vines, near a village called " Zabourka," at twenty minutes to two. Here we reposed for an hour, and then began to descend into the valley of Nahr el Salib, upon emerging from which we scrambled and clambered over an ascent, covered with calcined stones and scoria, to Ahtouta.

Again the sun went down in a sea of gold azure and glory, and lighted up with his departing rays the loveliest of prospects. A little

outside of the village of Ahtouta, I fou[nd a]
beautiful stone sarcophagus with two com[part]
ments on each side, and one on each end, [orna]
mented with well executed rosettes and pen[dant]
wreaths of roses. It was open, and its c[over]
lay by the road side. I had seen many s[uch]
sarcophagi near Deir el Kalaä, but none so [well]
executed as this one, which seems to be Gr[eek.]
It had as usual no inscription. It is surrou[nd]
ed by scoria and lava, and looks as if it [had]
stood there previous to the irruption of [the]
fiery flood.

I now rode on through mulberry and [other]
gardens to the village, and took up my bivou[ac]
under a superb Valonia oak, in the middle [of]
the place; the sheiks and villagers all throngi[ng]
around the " Elchi Bey," (foreign lord,) as th[ey]
called me. I treated the sheiks with coff[ee,]
they seating themselves respectfully at a d[is]
tance from my carpets, and regaling me in th[eir]
turn with a delicious kind of sweet Champag[ne]
grapes, figs, and melons.

We had not been long acquainted with ea[ch]

other ere they began to tell me, in a very mysterious manner, of a large hidden treasure in the neighbourhood, which many had seen, but could not get at for the large rocks which lay over it. They had no doubt that the " Elchi" was a " Mugrebbin," (magician,) and that he could cause the rocks to move on one side, and lay open the treasure to their rapacity. I affected to encourage the idea, in order to see to what lengths their credulity would go, and told them that if they would provide men, ropes, and poles, I could, without having recourse to the black art, remove all the obstacles, and get at the desired object; but I stipulated that one half of the whole treasure should be mine, and that their Excellencies the Sheiks should pay all the expenses of the transaction. They promised faithfully to obey me in all things, and appeared quite satisfied that the morrow's sun would put them in possession of untold gold. I was not quite so sanguine, having before heard of Arab covetousness, and propensity to believe in the marvellous.

We supped cordially together upon soup
roast mutton, which my servant prepared,
all retired to our repose; they to their ho
and I to my carpet. In the night time, I
ever, one of my friends stole quietly up to
bivouack, probably with the design of pilfe
any stray article of my baggage; but P
was too vigilant to permit of a near approac
his master's person, and springing up from
feet where he lay, seized the astonished A
by the throat, who nearly fainted from ap
hension. I was awake all the time, and w
I thought the intruder was sufficiently punis
by his panic, called my faithful guardian
and released the trembling Arab from his a
ward posture. The brightness of the mo
beams as they penetrated through the th
foliage of the tree over my head and fell
rectly upon me, prevented me from sleepi
and appeared to have the same effect upon t
Arabs, all of whom were in motion long bef
daylight. I have since had occasion to c
serve the custom of very early rising throug
out my journeys.

October 9.—At half-past six o'clock I set off on foot, accompanied by one of the sheiks, in search of the hidden treasure, followed by many of the most notable among the villagers; but, alas! the vanity of human expectations! We found nothing but old broken tombs, similar to those of Deir el Kalaā, and primitive blocks of limestone. I fear that I fell very low in the worthy sheik's estimation, when I assured him, with all the gravity I could assume, that I did not believe in the existence of any treasure in that spot, but that a friend of mine, who had possession of Solomon's ring, (a great and renowned talisman) should come and examine the ground more minutely.

In the neighbourhood of these old tombs there are some vestiges of an ancient town, probably Greek or Phœnician.

I now returned towards the village, and taking a cordial leave of my Arab friends, mounted my trusty mule, and proceeded towards Facra, my road leading through delightful forests of young oaks, shady and verdant slopes, and clear brooks. As I ascended the heights in my front, I took leave, by degrees, of the region of vegetation, and entered that of stone and water, passing by a rapid red stream, (by the side of which ran a clear brook,) and a ruined aqueduct on my left hand, and reaching the little village of Facra, consisting of a few huts, at about eight o'clock: here, by the side of a mountain stream, in a deep dell, amid plane-trees, grazed at their ease herds of horned cattle and camels. Crossing this dell, and continuing to ascend the craggy heights before me, I suddenly came upon the ruins of the temples of Facra, seated amid a range of (what appeared to me to be) basaltic rocks. The temples seem to have been five in number, four of which are of the Doric, and one of the Corinthian order.

While rambling about among these ruins, I flushed several covies of partridges, but all at too great a distance to be attainable by my short double-barrelled gun. My servant Jiaccomo discovered, in the face of one of the cliffs, an excavation, which, upon entering, we found to be a tomb. It was a cave, about five feet high

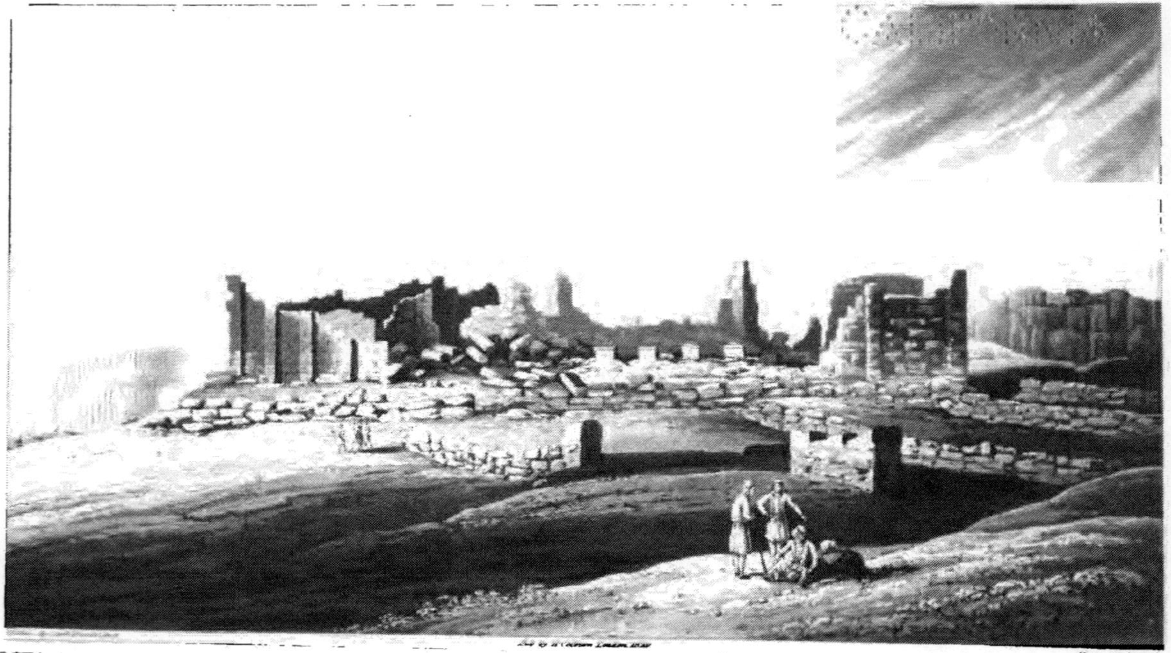

and twelve long, containing four cells for bodies, one on each side, and two across the farther end, lying parallel to each other. The doorway was very perfect; the hole in which the pivot of the door turned was still very visible, as likewise the chambers cut to receive the bolt or lock. I sat some time in this tomb, enjoying much the cool shade which it afforded. We breakfasted under a tree, in front of the principal temple, of which I made a rough sketch.

This temple was of the Corinthian order; five pedestals and several capitals of columns denote its former beauty. There was an anti-temple of the Doric order, part of whose front, ornamented with pilasters and frieze, still remains. The façade of the anti-temple is forty-four paces in length, and about thirty feet in height. These beautiful structures have been totally destroyed, by what means I know not; but if this be, as I suppose, a volcanic region, and if the singularly formed rocks among which the ruins stand, be, as I imagine, basaltic, perhaps the solution of the problem is sufficiently **easy**. These rocks are of a greyish colour, in **truncated** and columniated masses; the truncated **ends** are curiously marked with a sort of star, **the** columns are irregular and dissimilar, and are **all** fluted, each flute increasing in breadth as **it** approaches the base of the column. **When** struck, they yield a kind of metallic sound; **the** edges of the flutes are as sharp as knives. I am not sufficient geologist to determine whether this may be a volcanic or a calcareous formation. The stone with which the temples are constructed is grey in colour, and marked all over and throughout with black circular specks.

About a quarter of an hour's walk from the principal temple, towards the sea, there is a large square tower, which has apparently been surmounted by a canopy supported by Doric columns, many of which are lying about near it. On its north side is a doorway, ornamented with a Doric cornice and frieze. On the right hand, upon a corner stone, is a Greek inscription, which I copied;* it has in its interior, flights

*See notes.

of steps leading upwards and downwards alternately, all round the building. In the centre, upon the ground-floor, is a deep arched vault, into which I penetrated, as far as I dared; but having no light, could not discover for what purpose it had been constructed; I concluded that it was a tomb. There is likewise near the tower a well of ancient construction, the top of which was curiously closed by a mass of white marble, cut so as to fill up its mouth.

As I was anxious to reach Akoura for this night's halting-place, I did not deem it prudent to remain much longer here, lest I should be benighted in some of the most dreary parts of the Gebbail Sennin, as the loftiest region of this mountain is called. At 12. 30. therefore, I set off for Akoura, and at 1. 30. reached a great natural curiosity, an immense arch in the rock, under which the river of milk (Nahr el Leben) runs. This makes a complete bridge across a deep ravine. The arch is about one hundred feet in span, and seventy in height from the bed of the river. I descended, on foot, a rugged precipice into the bed of the stream, and made a very rough drawing of it. My mules and servants crossed over the bridge above my head, while I clambered over the opposite cliffs, and rejoined them.

We next came to Nahr el Ahssa, and had a weary ride over the Gebbail Sennin. Suddenly, towards sunset, we obtained a view of the plains of the Bakaa Motooalis and the Anti-Lebanon. We now found that we had lost our way, and that we had got too far to the eastward. We were in a perfectly desert region, without vegetation or water, excepting in one spot, where there was a circular stagnant pool, upon the margin of which we observed the traces of swines' feet; but this water was only fit for such cattle as the wild herd. We wandered on, not exactly knowing what to do, when suddenly we reached the edge of an immense precipice of several thousand feet; beneath us lay two villages of Metooali Turks. These said Metooali are all brigands. We were in an awkward predicament, between the chance of being plun-

A SKETCH OF THE NATURAL BRIDGE OVER
NAHR-EL-LEBEN.

dered, if we descended, (supposing such a thing possible,) and of passing a wretched night, without water or any thing to eat, for ourselves and cattle. We could find no road, and the precipice was too deep and dangerous to be descended. We saw, indeed, some wild swine, and Jiaccomo took his gun, and went with Ponto in pursuit of them, hoping to get us some pork for supper. They were too wild to be approached; and we went supperless to our bivouack. My servants were under great apprehension of the Metooali; but, nevertheless, they soon fell fast asleep, leaving me and Ponto to watch over them.

I was disturbed about midnight by a kind of snuffling, grunting sound; and grasping my gun, I aroused my servants, and Ponto; the dog darted forward, and we soon saw a drove of swine making off as fast as they could towards the pool of water before mentioned. The muleteer was very much terrified, making sure that the Metooali had fallen upon our melancholy bivouack. It is difficult to give an accurate idea of the beauty of the moon in this climate, and of the nature of the cold solitary scenery which she lighted up with her pale rays.

October 10.—We arose from our lair before the sun, and descended, in a circuitous direction, to the right of the precipice, in search of a road. As we proceeded we found abundance of indigenous cypresses, but much stunted and disfigured by the cold and rough winds of the mountain; we likewise found a kind of yellow plum, and saw all around us quantities of partridges; but all were too wild to suffer us to get within shot of them.

We at length found a road, which conducted us down a deep valley, and through some fields of maize, to the Metooali village of Naitra. These people are a set of schismatical Mussulmans, and are equally hated and dreaded both by the true believers and the Christians. They are by profession herdsmen and robbers. We were perhaps fortunate, in our cold and comfortless lodging of last night; for had we succeeded in reaching Naitra, we should, in all probability, have been ill treated and robbed.

We reached the village at eight o'clock, and had a conference with some of the Metooali, who looked with a longing eye at my baggage, and seemed inclined to dispute my farther progress. I was, however, too well armed, as were likewise my attendants, to be in much fear upon that score; and suddenly breaking from them, proceeded to a large walnut-tree, where I dismounted, and prepared for breakfasting. On my left hand, separated from Naitra by a river, stood the village of Afka.

We engaged, meanwhile, a guide to conduct us on to Akoura; and my man Jiaccomo suffered himself to be prevailed upon to pay him half of his fare beforehand, notwithstanding all my arguments to the contrary.

While I was at breakfast, I was much amused at observing the respect with which the inferior villagers approached and kissed the hand of a green-turbaned, dirty-looking Metooali, who received their homages upon the flat roof of his wretched hovel, with as much grace and dignity as if he had been bred in the most polite courts of the East. It is curious to observe the great superiority of manners and appearance which distinguishes the Mussulmans of all denominations and ranks, from the Christian Rayas.

The people of Naitra had lately been visited with the vengeance of the Emir Beshir, for the murder of a German traveller last year.

The Prince, who has lately embraced the Christian religion, but is in reality a Druse, governs the mountain with much vigour, and has done much to insure the safety of travellers in his dominions. He beheaded all the persons concerned in the murder, and cut down all the mulberry-trees of the villages of the Metooali. However much I admire the policy of the decapitation, still I must question that of destroying the mulberry-trees, which, by preventing the barbarians from attending to a lucrative and peaceful employment, necessarily threw them again into brigandage; and, in consequence thereof, there is at this moment a gang of robbers belonging to Naitra and Afka, who are proscribed and hunted by the satellites of the Emir, and who dare not enter their homes. This information, which we gathered from the Metooali themselves, was none of the most pleasing, and rather alarmed my attendants, who, being Christians, fear the ferocity and courage of the Mussulmans in a most ludicrous degree.

I left Naitra at 9. 30. and set off for Akoura with my Metooali guide, who, having been paid half his hire beforehand, soon took an opportunity to desert us; going down to a large walnut-tree on our left hand, under pretence of purchasing some of its fruit to sell at Akoura. It was in vain that I shouted after him; he would not return to us. We soon after met a large party of the Emir's people, collecting the miri in the Metooali district. These were Arab Christians; and I own I did feel a great degree of pleasure upon beholding, in a Mussulman country, the supremacy of the Christian power.

The Emir is tributary, however, to the Pasha

of Acre, and this miri is collected, nominally, for the Pasha's treasury; but the Emir takes care, when he is called upon to levy money for the Pasha, to appropriate large sums to his own use. Thus, if he be called upon by the Pasha Abdallah to send him fifteen thousand purses, he will perhaps, under pretence of this mandate, levy twenty-five thousand, and account only to himself for the difference. It is manifest, therefore, that the Christian Arabs of Mount Lebanon do not gain much, in a pecuniary way, in being governed by a prince of their own faith; on the contrary, I believe them to be much more oppressed by the Emir Beshir, than the inhabitants of the plains are by the Turks; for they have to pay both Pasha and Emir. Nevertheless, the state of freedom incident to a mountain life; the absence of Turks; the enjoyment, in perfect security of their own religious rites; the primitive government of their own sheiks; their lovely scenery and fine air, lend a charm to their existence, unknown to the degraded and servile population of the pashalicks of the plains.

As we approached Akoura, we came to the source of a river of that name, the water of which gushed out under a natural arch in the rock, which, like that of Nahr el Leben, forms a bridge over which the road runs. This arch is close upon the side of a lofty and remarkably-formed mountain, which is of a conical form, supported, as it were, by immense buttresses.

We reached Akoura at 11. 20. This is a small Christian town, having a manufactory of silk. Here we found abundance of walnut-trees; this circumstance making the bad faith of our Metooali guide more evident. We halted under the friendly shade, and dined upon fruit and eggs, as we could not procure any meat, it being a fast-day.

Here I was again surrounded by the Arabs, whose curiosity was excited by the appearance of a stranger among them. One of the sheiks showed me a piece of stone which contained gold; it was extremely heavy, and was found, as he informed me, in the neighbouring mountain before alluded to. He said it was commonly found there, but did not know what it contained. When I told him that it was gold, he appeared delighted, but would not allow me to carry off the stone, his cupidity being now aroused.

At half-past two we left Akoura, and ascended a volcanic region, inhabited by Metooali and Bedouin Arabs; the former seemed to be all employed in ploughing up the ground, each of them being armed up to the teeth, and looking as fierce and savage as possible. The Bedouins, with their black tents of camel's hair, their flocks and herds, were peaceably strolling about upon the plains, which every now and then are found upon the loftiest regions of Mount Lebanon.

My attendants were in a state of alarm all this while, and kept calling to me to be upon my guard. I never saw such a timid race as these Christians of Mount Lebanon; the very sight of a Turk or Bedouin creates all sorts of terrors in their breasts. Indeed, the ferocious manners of the Metooali, and the abusive language they indulge in towards the Christians, are such as render them objects at once of dread and detestation; while the pilfering disposition of the Bedouin always makes him the object of suspicion and disgust.

The ground in this region was covered with large flat square blocks of black shining stone, having its surface full of little holes, all nearly of equal depth. I imagined this to be lava, or basalt. Towards sunset, we found near a little spring, upon a large smiling plain, two Metooali Turks of apparent rank, who saluted us as we passed. I desired Jiaccomo to halt, and find out who they were, and try to gain information from them respecting our route; as we were unable to procure a guide at Akoura, for fear of the Metooali. One of the Turks proved to be the Emir of Baalbeck, who was on his way to Tripoli. He afterwards joined our cavalcade, and offered to be our guide as far as our routes coincided. I had not, however, much relish for his society, more especially as I knew he would expect a present at parting; my valise contained nothing but what was necessary to myself; and I have not sufficient regard for the natives of the East, to expose myself to inconvenience, for the sake of purchasing their good opinion of my generosity; add to this, the Emir was a Metooali, and I did not feel quite sure of his good faith. I declined, as politely as I could, his offers of service, and pushing on as fast as possible, bade him good evening.

My way still led over a green plain, well watered by clear streams. The mountaineers understand the art of irrigation, and convey the water in all directions through little channels.

Before the sun set we caught a fine view of the sea and of Tripoli, far down below us, a little more to the north-west than our route.

We now began to descend, among dwarf cypresses, towards Nahr el Ahb, the villages of Lacklouk and Tanurin, with their convents, amid walnut-trees beneath us to the left hand.

I had hoped to reach Bsherri this night; but we were overtaken by the darkness a long way from that town, and, to all appearances, were likely to pass another comfortless night, with nothing to eat, amid the rocks and wild swine. We were fortunate enough, however, to find a Christian Arab herdsman's hut about nine o'clock; and here we resolved upon halting for the night. The Arabs came out very kindly and assisted me to dismount, carrying my arms into the hut, and leaving it entirely at my disposal. I did not choose to enter, dreading the vermin with which these poor people abound, but prepared my bivouack close to their fire outside. We had nothing to eat; but our Arab host had plenty of Indian corn, which indeed he cultivated for his goats. The heads of this corn he roasted in the fire, and, when thus dressed, they are by no means disagreeable food. 1 desired Jiaccomo, however, to get some milk, and see if he could not make a kind of hot mess for our supper. Milk there was none, it having been all sold that evening to the people of the neighbouring town of Harrissa. The Arabs endeavoured to get us some honey, and shouted out to their neighbours, on the opposite side of the valley, to bring us some; but we could not procure any.* We had fortunately a few onions in the saddle-bags, and some very stale bread, which we had got at Solima. With these ingredients, and some salt and pepper, we made a sort of stewed mess, which, although it was none of the most savoury, was hot and comfortable to our hungry stomachs. The Arab had likewise a sort of bread made of lentils, which was not badly flavoured.

OCTOBER 11.—I broke up our bivouack at five in the morning, and engaging our host as a guide to take us on to the Cedars, proceeded in search of some supposed antiquities, which he told us were near our route. He related a long story about a Frank Mugrebbin who had visited these ruins, and after writing something in unknown characters, in a mysterious-looking

* This custom of hailing each other from the tops of the mountains is very prevalent throughout the district of Lebanon, and the effect of the human voice, when so exerted in these lofty regions, is very extraordinary.

book, had thrown the said book upon the top of a high rock, where it still was to be seen. I regret to say, that I could discover neither ruins or book.

We ascended a tedious mountain until seven o'clock, when we saw very plainly Tripoli and its neighbouring white cliffs. At thirty-five minutes past nine, we caught the first view of the Cedars of Mount Lebanon.

At nine, we crossed the three separate sources of the Nahr el Hadisha, and saw Hosroun and Bsherri, both beautifully situated upon the tops of hills amid trees and streams, but considerably below us on our left. The irrigation of the corn and grass-fields in this quarter is most carefully attended to, and skilfully managed by the Arab peasant.

We rode wearily on over hill and dale; and after crossing the deep ravine of the Hadisha, and mounting the opposite heights, we reached, at forty-five minutes past ten, the Cedars. These celebrated trees are seated upon an elevated plain, sloping down towards Bsherri, but bounded towards the north-east and south by a lofty chain of mountains, which are perfectly destitute of vegetation, save here and there a straggling cedar. They form a thick black-looking mass or clump, and from the outside do not fulfil the expectation of the traveller who has made so weary a journey to come and visit them. Upon entering the clump, however, he is much struck by the imposing grandeur and venerable appearance of the largest of the trees, which may be in number four. Many hundreds of travellers have inscribed their names upon them, and have very much injured their beauty by ripping off large pieces of the bark, in order to clear away a space upon which to write these mementoes of their travels. I spread my carpets under the largest of the group, which divides itself into five ramifications immediately above the ground. Here, invoking the *genius loci*, I wrote a letter to my mother, and made a sketch of a fine cedar opposite to me. Poor Jiaccomo, Ponto, the muleteer, the guide, and the mules, were all knocked up, and sleeping round about me on the ground. I inscribed my name in the same place with that of my friend Mr. Maddox, who had been here three years ago, and then proceeded to knock down some of the cones from the trees to give to my friends in Europe. These celebrated cedars have been measured over and over again by various travellers, each of whom has given a different estimate of their size. I did not take this trouble, nor did I think it worth the while. They certainly are not at all like the cedars which we have seen in Europe, but bear a resemblance to some of the larger of the pine tribe.

It had been my intention to push on, this day, over the high mountain to the eastward, and to sleep at Ainette, at its south-east foot; but my cattle and attendants were too weary to be able to undertake the task of ascending the heights. I resolved therefore upon reposing beneath the classic shade of the venerable cedars for some hours, and then to descend to the Frank convent at Bsherri, and pass our night there. Accordingly, after having breakfasted and reposed until half past two, we set out for the Carmelite Convent at Bsherri, and descended a very rough and dangerous road, passing by an ancient tomb excavated in the rock on our right hand, and still pursuing our winding descent. Leaving the town on the right, we proceeded towards the valley of the Hadisha with its green meadows in the bottom full of flocks and herds. Turning our faces towards the east, we wound along a tedious ascent to the foot of a high sandy mountain, and passing under a trellice of vines, we reached, at fifty minutes past four, the convent, or rather hermitage, cut out in the solid rock. Here we were kindly received by a venerable but garrulous old Carmelite friar, a Neapolitan, and tolerably lodged. I sent out to purchase a kid, resolving to make merry, and to forget our two last days' fasting.

The view from the little terrace in front of the hermitage, arched over by the vines, was beautiful beyond description. The river Hadisha forces itself down through a deep ravine, the sides of which are covered with trees, and verdure. This ravine is so deep, that the eye does not penetrate through the dark blue haze which seems to veil its mysteries. The mountains decrease gradually in size as they approach the sea, and are clothed with forests and studded with convents, more particularly that of Cannobine, the residence of the Maronite patriarch. As you face the sea, you have on your left hand the village of Hosroun, perched upon the top of a conical hill, which rises out of the valley of the Hadisha, and on the right front the town of Bsherri, seated on the side of the mountain, and embosomed amid mulberry plantations and large walnut-trees; in your rear are the loftiest peaks in this part of the range of Mount Lebanon. I enjoyed very much the sunsetting, and the beauty of the evening, sipping coffee with the good old hermit upon my carpets spread beneath the rich clustering vines. We supped together most gloriously upon kid, my friend, old Ponto, seeming to enjoy very much the return to animal food. There were two dormitories in the hermitage, in one of which I reposed very comfortably.

OCTOBER 12.—I arose before the sun, but had to wait a long time for a guide, for arrack, bread, &c. &c. At 6. 30. however we set off, being provided with every thing; but I did not like the physiognomy of the guide, who was an ill-favoured and insolent-looking Metooali Turk, belonging to one of the villages in the Bakaa. We passed the Cedars at eight, and began to ascend the crest of Mount Lebanon; but ere we had got half-way up, the guide refused to go on, unless he were paid thirteen piastres (his agreement being for three). The pretext for this attempted extortion was, that Mr. Maddox had paid that sum to each of his four guides, when he crossed the mountain in 1824; but then the snow was several feet deep, and there was no road to be seen. I desired that he might be told that I did not need his assistance, that the road lay before me, and that I could not possibly mistake it; that if he were dissatisfied he might return to Bsherri. He became extremely insolent and vociferous, and quarrelled very much with the muckrow about some bread which he had bought of him, indeed he would not let the muckrow proceed with the baggage until he had paid him more than the value of the bread he had purchased of him; the muckrow was quite a youth, and was afraid of the Metooali, so that I was obliged to menace him, by cocking my gun and pointing it at his head, ere he would rid us of his society. At length he went away, and we hoped to see no more of him.

We reached the top of the mountain at 9. 50. and had a fine view of the Bakaa, and the lofty range of Anti-Libanus, to the east and southeast; and of the sea, to the westward. On our descent towards Ainette, we met several droves of mules and asses going to Tripoli and Bsherri, from Damascus and the Bakaa. We were, to our great annoyance, overtaken by our quondam guide, who, by a footpath, came suddenly upon us, and began throwing stones and abusing us.

A little lower down we came to a party of Arabs, who were sitting by a spring refreshing themselves. The guide, upon seeing them, ran on, and seizing one of their muskets, began to threaten us, and endeavoured to raise the Arabs against us, and prevent our passing by. I however rode against him and attempted to force the way; but he seized the bridle of the mule, and pointed the musket at my head. I had time enough to observe that the pan was open; and laughing in his face, beat down the muzzle of his musket, and pushed him on one side. The Arabs, meanwhile, had stopped my servant and the baggage, and thus I was obliged to halt and hold a parley with them. They began by saying that the Metooali had called upon them for justice, and that they would see justice done before they would suffer me to depart.

I now began to think that I had indeed fallen among the thieves, and that the justice they intended would be done upon my purse and baggage, if not upon my person. Assuming, therefore, as much appearance of haughtiness and determination as I could, and desiring my followers to be upon their guard, I told the Arabs that I did not acknowledge their right to interfere with me; that I was resolved to oppose force to force if any should be attempted against me; that the guide had broken his contract, by refusing to conduct me more than half-way, without an increase of his stipulated reward; that as he had not fulfilled his agreement, so I was at liberty likewise not to fulfil mine, and that therefore I was resolved upon not giving him a para; that this was justice, and that I asked for nothing more at their hands. I told them I was an English officer, and that any insult or injury I might sustain from them, would be surely followed by instant punishment; and that the Emir Beshir had lately given a dreadful instance of his vengeance for a similar outrage, as they all well knew. I referred them to Jiaccomo for an account of the transaction, and observed, that as he was himself an Arab, it was not likely he should attempt to deceive them in this matter, but would tell them the whole merits of the case.

My harangue produced the desired effect; the two principal persons of the party came up to me, and gave me fruit to eat, as a token of their designing to do me no harm. They said they knew the guide to be a man of bad character, and that he was mad; that if I desired it, they would chastise him and let him go. I did not wish to do this, being apprehensive of his exercising a greater influence among his own people lower down, who might not be so well disposed towards me as the Arabs were, and that I might be ill-treated, or perhaps murdered by them. I said, that as he was mad, he was an object of compassion and not of resentment; and that, in consideration of his calamity, I would give him the three piastres to which he would have been entitled, had he performed his agreement.

The Metooali, meanwhile, was gnashing his teeth and foaming at the mouth from rage and vexation; he refused indignantly the three piastres; and making a very contemptuous motion to Jiaccomo, as he proffered him the money, dashed off down the side of the mountain, and we saw no more of him.

The Arabs now took their leave with many compliments, and offers of protection as far as Baalbeck, should I feel any apprehension upon the score of the guide. I declined their offer as graciously as I could, and continuing my route, reached the ruined and deserted village of Ainette at 11. 40. Here, under a splendid walnut-tree by the side of a clear and rapid stream, I dined and reposed until 12. 30.; when I set off for Deir el Akmar, passing through low woods of Valonia oak, wild plum, and dwarf oak, seeing great quantities of red-legged partridges, but not liking to discharge my gun, which was loaded with ball for the Metooali.

The descent became gradually gentler, over mountainets and slopes, full of herds and Metooali, (ill-looking and dirty people,) of whom we purchased some cheese. As I approached Deir el Akmar, I observed some curious ancient cisterns. The ruins of a small Corinthian temple in the village are converted into a Greek church and the abode of the curate; there are two pilasters in the façade still perfect. Here I alighted at 3. 15.; my cattle being too tired to proceed on to Baalbeck, and there being no good halting-place on the road.

I took up my quarters upon the top of the ruined temple, from whence I had a fine view of Baalbeck to the south-east. Here I received the visits of the curate and the principal inhabitants, among the rest, an amazingly fine-looking Arab sheik, who was sent down here by the Emir Beshir, to collect the miri. I was delighted to see the air of superiority with which he received the Metoaali chiefs, who came up to my terrace, to pay their respects to me, and their money to the Emir's deputy. He weighed all their adlees (golden ducats) carefully in his hand; and whenever he felt doubtful of their being good, always referred to me for my opinion. I gave them all coffee, and such refreshments as I had to offer them.

While I was squatting down among them, Mr. Bird, one of the American missionaries, who was on his way from Baalbeck to Bsherri, came upon the terrace, having heard of my arrival. He was dressed à l'Arabe, and was accompanied by several of the young sheiks of the mountains. I invited him to stay and share my supper and bivouack, and allowed him to copy my Facra inscriptions. We had a long, and to me a very interesting conversation, respecting the success of the missions, which seems to fall very short of the expectations formed by the over sanguine promoters of the scheme in England and America; indeed, they do not appear to have made any but doubtful converts, and seem to be a good deal persecuted by the Christian patriarchs, who have excommunicated all those of their several communions who hold any correspondence with the missionaries. We spread our carpets by the side of each other, and retired to our repose at an early hour. The bright moon, the biting fleas, for they reached us even here;

the barking curs, some of whom, attracted by the smell of our provisions, clambered up to our bivouack, and battled away with Ponto, kept me awake all the night long. Mr. Bird left me about the middle of the night.

CHAPTER II.

Departure from Deir el Akmar.—Remarkable excavation.—Corinthian column.—Baalbeck.—Description of the ruins.—River Djoush.—Visit from the Emir's people.—Conduct of Jiaccomo.—Behaviour of Muleteer.—Reference to Cogia Bashi.—Magisterial proceedings.—New arrangements.—Curiosity of the populace, and political conversation.—Fresh embarrassments.—Fracas among the natives.—Good conduct of Greek curate.—Departure from Baalbeck.—Zurgaia—Bivouack.—Zerbdeni.—Souk, and antiquities.—Dumar.—View of Damascus.—Entrance into the city.—Capuchin convent.—Terra Santa.—M. Bodin.—Description of Damascus.—Lazarites.—Plague.—Departure from Damascus.—Dimass.—Apprehensions of ambuscade.—Khan el Margi.—Ascent of Mount Lebanon.—Druses.—Khan el Lassan and bivouack.—Descent towards Bairout.—Arrival at Bairout.

OCTOBER 13.—I arose before daylight, and set off at five o'clock for Baalbeck, passing by a remarkable excavation, partly arched over, and having a stone tomb at either end, at fifteen minutes past five. At half-past six, I came to a beautiful Corinthian column, to the right of the road; it is about sixty feet in height, and is composed of seventeen blocks of marble, having a tablet on its north side, where probably was once an inscription. On its capital sat a huge black eagle, which flew away when I presented my gun at him.

At 8.40. I reached the outer wall of the stupendous temple of Baalbeck, and breakfasted under a fine walnut-tree, close to a clear stream which bathes its walls. While breakfast was preparing, I wandered through an immense arched passage one hundred and sixty paces in length, having another passage of equal dimensions intersecting it in the middle. At one hundred and twenty paces from the entrance, I found a large fragment of a red granite column. After breakfast, I rode round the east end of the walls to the Greek curate's house, in the wretched and half-ruined Turkish town of Baalbeck, observing, as I went, several inverted inscriptions, pedestals of statues, cornices, &c. &c. thrust, without any regard to order, into the walls of the Turkish fortress which surrounds the temple. My host was a decent young man, who received me with great civility, and gave me part of his only room upon the ground-floor, in a kind of court-yard, on one side of which was his chapel.

I spent the forenoon in visiting and examining the stupendous ruins of the temple. These ruins have been well described by Maundrell, in his curious and correct work, and beautifully illustrated by Wood and Dawkins. I shall nevertheless endeavour to show what they are at present, and what was the impression they made upon my mind, claiming all indulgence at the hands of the reader for any incorrect architectural terms of which I may make use.

To begin with the situation of Baalbeck, I would say, that it is seated upon a gentle eminence, near the north-eastern extremity of the plain of the Bakaā Metooalis, between the ranges of Libanus and Anti-Libanus, but nearer to the latter than to the former mountains. It is supposed to be the ancient Heliopolis of the Greeks. Its inhabitants are chiefly Metooali

Turks and Greek Christians; their chief is a Metooali Turk, having the title of Emir; its population may be about two thousand. It was once celebrated for the beauty and profligacy of its women; but at the present day, I should say that they were too ugly to be very profligate: the men are remarkable throughout Syria for their rapacity, insolence, and ferocity, and most travellers have had some cause to repent of having fallen into their hands. The remains of its beautiful Temple of the Sun, (or of Jupiter, I know not which,) may be classed among the finest monuments of antiquity. They are now surrounded, and screened partially from the view, by the ruins of a gigantic Turkish fortress, which indeed are of themselves extremely beautiful and imposing, and seem to have been constructed out of the materials of the temples which they surround. The principal temple appears to have had a portico in its front, and an anti-temple of the Corinthian order, of hexagonal shape, the walls of which are still adorned with pilastres, niches for statues, finely ornamented doors, and a highly-wrought entablature enriched with festoons. The pedestals of columns which still remain seem to indicate that this building was ornamented by a fine colonnade. Now follows a large quadrangular space, which is encumbered by the remains of a superb edifice. It seems likewise to have had its portico ornamented with statues.

The next remarkable object rivets the attention of the traveller; it is the remains of a gigantic colonnade, consisting of six lofty pillars of the Corinthian order, supporting their appropriate entablature: they appear to be between sixty and seventy feet in height, their diameter is about seven feet. Each shaft is composed of three blocks, very artificially joined together by means of iron pins and sockets in the centre of the column. To the left of this colonnade stand the most perfect of the remains. These consist of a quadrangular temple, surrounded by a peristyle of eight Corinthian columns in each front, and fifteen in each side, but few of these are now standing; their entablature is still very perfect, but nothing can exceed the beauty of the arched ceiling (composed of immense stones) which covers in this superb portico. It is divided into compartments, hexagonal and rhomboidal, the mouldings of which are carved in the most exquisite manner, and resemble the most beautiful designs upon lace or ivory. In each of the compartments are, in bas relief, heads and figures relating to the heathen mythology; such as Ganymede and the eagle, and that favourite topic of the ancients, Leda and the swan.

The entrance of the temple is blocked up, and totally screened from external view by a wall of Turkish construction, but is accessible through a hole near the ground, at the right-hand corner. I know not how to describe, in adequate terms, the beauty of its doorway, which is ornamented all round by a moulding of the richest and most exquisite specimen of the art of carving. On the upper sill of the doorway, in bas relief, is an eagle with extended wings, holding in his claw a Caduceus, and in his beak a long scroll, terminated by a festoon of flowers, each end of which is supported by a winged Genius. Unfortunately, the centre stone of the sill has sunk considerably below its level, and thus the unity of effect is destroyed.

In the interior of this temple are still the remains of a row of Corinthian pilasters against the walls, having between them a niche finely ornamented, and over each niche a well-wrought tabernacle. Above the pilasters runs a rich entablature. The roof of the temple (masses of whose reticulated ceiling still cover the ground) was supported by a double colonnade of the Corinthian order.

The barbarians do all that they can to destroy the superb remains of those arts which they can neither appreciate nor acquire. They dig into the heart of the lofty column, to get out the metal pins which connect its masses; they undermine the solid wall, which the hand of time has swept over in vain, in search of hidden treasures, and thus, year after year, these beautiful monuments of a polite and powerful people sink into utter ruin and oblivion, amid the barbarism and credulity of that hateful race, which seems to have been sent by Providence to chastise the pride and vices of civilized man, and to scourge him with a whip of scorpions, until that period shall arrive when the oppressor, in his turn, shall yield to the oppressed,—the victor to the vanquished.

Alas! how has the desolating hand of the Mussulman laid waste and depopulated the once fertile lands of Ionia and Phœnicia! Where are now the arts, the commerce, the splendid cities of the Grecian colonies? They are in the dust and the desert, and are trampled upon by the scornful foot of the arrogant barbarian!

About five hundred yards from the Temple of the Sun stand the relics of a lovely little circular temple. The order of the highly ornamented colonnade and entablature which encircles the building is Corinthian, but that of the inside is, in the lower compartment, Ionic, and in the upper, Corinthian. The shafts of the columns are all of one piece. At the present moment, nearly one half of the building has fallen down, and its fane is now usurped by a shrine dedicated to the Panagia, (Virgin,) and here the Greek Christians sometimes celebrate their religious rites. The half-ruined, miserable Turkish town presents nothing remarkable, save a Doric column, having upon one of its sides a grooved channel, and upon its capital a small basin or reservoir. It seems to have been constructed for the purpose of raising water to some given height. (There are many similar contrivances in Roumelia and Anatolia, but more barbarous.)

The town is still partly encompassed by a wall of apparently Turkish construction, being full of columns, thrust in endways, broken cornices, capitals, and inscriptions inverted, one of which near the gate, on the south side, I copied. There are near the walls several curious caverns and excavations in the rock, some of which, no doubt, are quarries. About three quarters of a mile to the south-east is the source of the river Djoush, which gushes out of the ground into a sort of basin. Near to this are some remains of Roman or Greek baths, and the ruins of a Turkish mosque.

The Moslem generally attribute the construction of the temples of Baalbeck to Solomon, who they believe to have been a great magician; he is said likewise to have built Palmyra or Tadmor; but it seems to be more rational to attribute Corinthian and Ionic structures to the Greeks, or to the Romans of the Byzantine empire. "Ælius Antoninus Pius built a temple of Jupiter at Heliopolis, near Libanus in Phœnicia;" and antiquarians seem inclined to give him the credit of these beautiful temples of Baalbeck.

On my return from the source of the Djoush, which I visited after I had examined the temples, I made a rough sketch of the ruins and the town, from a height to the left; but the wind was so violent, that I could hardly hold my book. When I had completed my little

tour of the walls, I returned to the curate's house, inviting him to sup with me.

In the evening my quarters were invaded by almost all the male population of the town, who came to look at the Frank traveller (Frangi); they were generally very civil and respectful, but extremely dirty people, abounding with vermin and *ill smells*. Later in the evening, some of the Emir's people came, and began to sound my servant as to the probability of my making the customary present to the Emir, who was absent. I had previously told Jiaccomo of my determination to resist this extortion, and had instructed him what to say, in the event of its being demanded of me. He therefore, to quote his own words, used " le parole forte," informing them that I had a firman from the Sultan; that I was a person of rank and influence; that I knew the Pasha of Tripoli; was going to the Pasha of Damascus and the Emir Beshir; that I had expressed to him my determination upon this point, and that I would only yield to force, which they had better beware how they made use of against me; that, as a Frank traveller with a firman, I had the Sultan's permission to visit every spot in his empire, should I think fit so to do, and that the Elchi Bey (ambassador) at Constantinople, as well as the two Pashas before mentioned, and the Emir Beshir, would be sure to avenge any insult offered to my person. During all this conversation, I was employed in writing up my journal, from the notes in my pocket-book, but lending an attentive ear and eye to what was passing.

These arguments seemed to stagger their resolution; they consulted awhile together, and at length wished me a good night, saying we should see on the morrow how it would be. I had, however, no firman, but merely a passport from Mr. Stratford Canning, endorsed by the proper Turkish authorities. I knew that there was no probability that any Turk in the town could read Turkish, and that very few, if any, knew a firman from any other document: I was therefore under no apprehension of the fraud's being discovered. I had seen, at Athens, the utter inability of the Pasha's Selictar to read a firman which was put into his hands, and the stupid gaze with which he regarded the tourra* of the Sultan: I did not expect therefore to find much more literary acquirement among the barbarous Metooalis of the Bakaā, than among the polite Turks of Stambool; but in the end, I had no occasion to put their learning to the proof.

Wearied as I was with my day's ramble, I could get no rest all night for the fleas, which seemed to have established their head-quarters in Baalbeck, and to be attracted simultaneously to the couch of their new comer.

October 14.—I arose before the dawn, to urge the preparations for departure; but, to my no small astonishment, found that my muleteer had decamped, after having induced Jiaccomo to pay his wages up to last night. I now found the evil consequences of paying Arabs beforehand. He had however forgotten to take with

* Signature of the Sultan.

him his mules and his musket; these I therefore instantly seized upon, resolving, *en dernier lieu,* to proceed on to Damascus without him. I despatched Jiaccomo in search of him, who returned with a message from him, saying that he had made a better bargain to go on to Zahle, a Christian town at the eastern foot of Mount Lebanon, from whence he could carry dried grapes, and figs, and corn, back to his native village, Buckfaya, and that he was afraid to go on to Damascus, dreading ill usage in that city. The fact was, he wanted to force me to increase his wages, by leaving me, as he thought, destitute of the means of continuing my journey.

I now sent for the Cogia Bashi, the only magistrate in the place, and told him how I was situated, and that by agreement made at Buckfaya, I had a right to take the mules on to Damascus, should I desire to do so; that all I required at his hands was justice, for which I hinted I was both willing and able to pay; and concluded by saying, that if he did not choose to force the muleteer to perform his contract,

I should proceed on my journey without waiting for him; and in the event of my passage being opposed, that I was resolved to shoot both the mules, as the only means left in my hands of punishing the muleteer for his treachery.

The Cogia Bashi said that I had reason on my side, and despatched some of his myrmidons to look for the delinquent, who was hidden somewhere in the town. We waited very patiently for him a long while; and as he did not make his appearance, the Cogia Bashi told me I was at liberty to depart without him, and that he would send some of his people with me to protect me, and bring the mules back from Damascus. I was upon the point of starting, when the muleteer arrived, accompanied by a great many others of his profession, Christians of Zahle, a very fierce and powerful tribe of Arabs; these men were all armed, and seemed resolved to screen the muleteer from punishment.

The Cogia Bashi was overawed, but still said that he would do justice; and proceeded to open his court upon the flat roof of a house near which we were standing. The Metooali grouped themselves on one side, and the Christians of Zahle on the other of the Cogia Bashi. I sat down a little in front of them all, backed by the Greeks of the town, having Jiaccomo, as my dragoman, on my right hand, on his feet, and Ponto on my left.

I now, through my interpreter, repeated all that I had before said to the Cogia Bashi, and insisted that the muleteer should be well bastinadoed for his breach of agreement, which punishment, I said, I would certainly inflict upon him with my own hands, should the Cogia Bashi suffer himself to be deterred from doing his duty, by the friends of the muleteer, who, I doubted not, were all as great rogues as himself.

The Cogia asked the culprit what he had to say in his defence; and upon receiving no answer, gave a nod to some of his people, who moved forward to seize the muleteer. The Christians of Zahle interposed to save him, and the Metooali retired; upon seeing this, I ran into the centre of the group and seized him by the arm, calling upon Jiaccomo to assist me in dragging him away. The men of Zahle again interposed to save their fellow mule-driver, and I was compelled to relinquish my grasp.

We all sat down again as tranquilly as if nothing had happened; and it appeared to me, that I should obtain no justice at the hands of the Cogia Bashi, who was evidently afraid to execute the law. I endeavoured again to rouse his spirit, by an appeal to his avarice, and greatly vaunted to him the justice and magnanimity of the Turkish magistrates in general;— all was in vain, and I was proceeding to mount the mules, and to set off in spite of all obstacles, when a Metooali offered to supply me with horses at a cheaper rate than I was paying for the mules.

This was too advantageous an offer to be refused, and I eagerly accepted it, as it seemed to be the only means of compromising the business with honour to myself. The mules were therefore unloaded, and the muleteer suffered to depart with a whole skin. He, however, had been heartily frightened, and perhaps abundantly punished by the anxiety he must have felt, while under the dread of the bastinado.

All being now seemingly arranged, the crowd gathered around me, and began to examine my arms, and every article of my equipment; they were more particularly struck with my English pistols, but could not be induced to believe that they would carry far. To gratify their curiosity, I fired one at a black mark upon a wall at some distance, and was lucky enough to strike it. The pistols were rifles, of which description of arm the Turks have no notion. They seemed all very much surprised and delighted.

One of the Greeks, a fine athletic fellow, armed up to the teeth, came forward and said, that the English were the only people in the world capable of making such weapons; and asked, when England would do something for the Greeks of Syria, as she was doing for those of the Morea.

I was surprised at his boldness in asking such a question among so many Mussulmans, and did not at first make him any reply; but he, observing my caution, bade me not be afraid; he said that the Greek and Arab Christians in Baalbeck were more than a match for the Metooali, who were indeed themselves as anxious for a change in the order of things as the Christians. I then told him that it depended entirely upon themselves, and upon their own good and courageous conduct, when the sympathies of Englishmen should be attracted towards the cause of the suffering Christians of Syria; but that if they really desired an improvement in their political state, they should depend upon their own exertions, and their own virtues, to obtain it for them, and not upon the aid of foreign arms, which perhaps might eventually be turned against themselves.

I now returned to my quarters at the Greek curate's, awaiting the arrival of the promised horses; but after waiting some time, and seeing nothing of them, I sent Jiaccomo to find out the Metooali who had engaged to furnish them immediately. After some delay the Metooali came, but said that the horses were out at grass, and could not be caught up until the morrow, unless I would raise the price which we had agreed upon. His drift was very clear, and he made quite sure of obliging me to pay nearly double the agreement, knowing that the muleteer had set off for Zahle, and that I was totally unprovided with the means of getting forward.

I was, however, resolved not to submit to any thing like imposition, foreseeing that should I once begin to show any symptoms of weakness, attempts of this sort would never end. I called the curate and several of the Greeks, to witness that I was willing to fulfil the agreement which had been made in sight of them all; but that I would not yield to such dishonest attempts upon my purse; that I would rather remain at Baalbeck until the arrival of the first caravan, than allow myself to be imposed upon. That I had frequently heard of the bad character of the inhabitants of Baalbeck, and that howsoever unwilling I might have been to place faith in such general reports, I was now too fully convinced of their being as bad as they were represented to be, and that their conduct to an unprotected stranger was unworthy of any but a set of robbers and ruffians. I then called for water, and washed the dust of Baalbeck off my hands and feet, in sight of the multitude, showing them the abhorrence and contempt with which I viewed their proceedings towards me.

The curate now began to take my part, observing that I had spoken " true words," and that the Greeks felt as I did, and would see me righted. Upon this an immense fracas between the armed ruffians took place in the court-yard; the Greeks all insisting upon my side, and the Metooali against me. Had I not known the nature of Oriental squabbles, I should have anticipated bloodshed; the flashing eyes, wagging beards, uplifted hands, and drawn handjars, all giving apparent indication of such a denouement. After a great deal of shouting, stamping, foaming, and spitting, the mob grew quieter, and all subsided into a calm; each individual sitting down upon the ground as if nothing had occurred. I was reclining meanwhile upon my carpet, watching the event, my man Jiaccomo looking very pale and uneasy at the storm which had so suddenly gathered around us. The Greek curate at length came to me, and informed me that the Metooali had been obliged, by the Cogia Bashi, to fulfil his agreement, and that I might expect the horses in a short time.

At fifteen minutes past ten, the cattle came, and I own that I did feel considerable delight in getting into my saddle, and taking leave of such a set of Philistines as these said *Baalbeckians*, unhurt in person or purse. I made, of course, a trifling present to the curate and the Cogia Bashi, both of whom seemed delighted with my generosity; indeed, to the honour of the curate be it spoken, I had some difficulty in persuading him to accept my gift, and even at last, it was only under the pretext of his distributing it in alms to the poor of his communion, that he would receive it. I saw no more of the Emir's people, nor did I hear another syllable about the present which he usually expects.

I had not been long on horseback, before I found that my horses were but miserable hacks, and that my guide knew nothing of the road. We steered across the plains about south, passing by many remarkable excavations, and an immense hewn stone of twenty feet in length. I apprehend that this stone was hewn out of the rock by the builders of the temples, as there are some others of immense size in the south-western wall, and some in the epistylia of the colonnade, equally large. To the right of the road, about a quarter of a mile from the quarry in which lies this large stone, is a small circular temple, less ruined than those of the city. I did not inspect it, as I was anxious to get as far away as possible from Baalbeck before dusk.

At noon I reached a very remarkable valley, or ravine of rocks, with a clear rivulet, and a miserable village, whose name I could not learn. We continued to follow the road, over an uncultivated region full of rocks, and came, at fifteen minutes past one, to another village; and then we began to ascend the lower range of the Anti-Lebanon, and lost our way repeatedly, from the total ignorance of the guide. The face of the country was often very pretty, and we saw many flocks of sheep and goats. We met a large caravan of camels, with their savage-looking Bedouin conductors. These people told us, that there was plague at Zurgaia and Damascus. I held a council in my own breast as to the expediency of abandoning the visit to the " Holy City" altogether, and cutting across to Zahle, and so back to Bairout; but I did not like to relinquish my project, having come thus far on my road; and I at last determined upon running all risks, and trusting entirely to that superintending Providence who had hitherto protected me in various countries and climates.

At four I reached the summit of the mountains, and began to descend by a good road into a most lovely valley, with a clear rivulet running rapidly through it towards the Backaā, its banks covered with aspen-poplars, and mulberry gardens. There is a good stone bridge over the river, where I halted to repose and to water my cattle, for about a quarter of an hour, when following the banks of the stream, we reached Zurgaia at forty minutes past four. We did not venture to enter this village, on account of the plague, but arranged our bivouack in a mulberry garden, close to the source of the rivulet, which gushed out of a hollow kind of basin in the ground with great rapidity; and here all the Turkish females came to wash their linen and to draw water.

October 15.—I arose before daybreak, and set off at half-past five, passing over a fertile and beautiful plain, bounded by high rocky mountains on each hand, and varied by gentle slopes and murmuring streams. At seven I reached the river Barrady, which I crossed at fifteen minutes past seven, and found upon its banks large groups of men, women, children, and cattle, who had established themselves here on account of the plague, which was raging at Zerbdeni; the mortality being equal to seventeen or eighteen daily, in a population of two thousand.

Zerbdeni is deliciously situated amid gardens, vineyards, purling brooks, green fields, and shady groves. What a pity that so lovely a spot should be made desolate by the pestilence! We were overtaken by some Turkish travellers, who belonged to Zerbdeni, and who, although they went unhesitatingly into the town, advised my avoiding it, which I carefully did, leaving it on my right hand about a mile distant, and passing through shady lanes, smiling gardens, vineyards, and clear brooks. I observed, with much pleasure, the care bestowed by the Turkish agriculturist in irrigating his soil, in which he seems to succeed admirably. I took leave gradually of this plain, and just where the road joins that from Damascus to Bairout, began, at ten o'clock, to clamber over brown and barren heights, and then to descend to a pretty fall of the river Barrady, the murmur of whose bright green waters had a most pleasing and lulling effect upon the ear and nerves. I now passed through high calcareous rocks, and observed a remarkable cavern on the right bank of the river.

At 10. 40. I reached Djissir el Souk. Here is a bridge with one arch; on the left hand, are six very remarkable caverns, and the façade of a temple or church with a flight of steps, all hewn in the rock. These are supposed to be the works of the primitive Christians, who fled to the deserts and caverns to escape persecution, and to celebrate, in solitude and safety, their mysterious rites. On crossing the bridge, you come to a sort of aqueduct hewn in the solid rock, which still conveys water.

About a quarter of an hour farther on, upon the right bank of the river, is a small village, and on the opposite bank, a little lower down, is the village of Souk. Upon the hill side, on the left bank, are some ancient remains, such as columns and architraves.

At 11. 10. I halted to breakfast under a mulberry-tree, near some remains of a temple; behind me was a little aqueduct with a cascade, which turned the wheel of a water-mill on my right hand. In the near side of the mill, I found a long Greek inscription, nearly perfect, which I copied. (See notes.)

At 12. 30. I set off again, and following the course of the river, reached Husseine at 12. 45. I now left the bank of the Barrady, and traversed a range of calcareous hills, towards Elgdidie, meeting some parties of Turks, among the rest, a ferocious-looking black Aga, followed by a splendid suite of Mamelukes. At 2. 15. I crossed a pretty tributary stream to the Barrady, full of watercresses and lilies.

We passed the village of Elgdidie at 2. 30. It is situated upon a conical hill on the left bank of the Barrady; the valley at its feet, through which the river rapidly runs, is full of trees and verdure. Hereabouts I met some more of the Turkish military, among others, a splendid-looking Aga of Spahis, armed up to the teeth, his lance being borne by a black slave. He had on either hand a little son; they were beautiful children; mounted upon handsome Arab horses. The contrast between his martial and even ferocious visage, and their lovely smiling countenances, was most strikingly beautiful. The Turks are remarkable for their tenderness to their young children, many instances of which, I have before had opportunities of observing.

I reached Djissir el Dumar (Djissir signifies bridge) at 4. 15.; it has two pretty arches, and is in good repair. Upon crossing it, I found many caravans of mules, and asses, and camels, and some parties of Turks, which latter were purifying and praying, prior to taking up their bivouack for the night, upon the bank of the stream. Leaving the river to my right hand, I passed over some high barren hills, and reached a remarkable Khubbe* at 5. The road now

* Khubbe, in Arabic, signifies a dome or cupola, one of which is generally erected over the tomb of some Santon or Sheik celebrated for his virtues.

led between high rocks, through which indeed it has been with much labour excavated, and suddenly terminating, opens upon one of the most lovely views I have ever beheld. At my feet, in an immense plain bounded by the mountains of the Haouran, embosomed in groves and gardens, watered by three branches of the Barrady, stood the noble city of Shem, or Damascus.* Twenty-one mosques, with their cupolas and minarets, embellish the prospect, and break the outline of buildings.

Exactly upon this spot where I now stood, nearly five centuries ago Mahomet halted, as he led his victorious forces to the conquest of Anatolia. He gazed upon the bewitching scenery before him, and doubtlessly longed for the repose and pleasures which such a city seemed to offer him; but suddenly recollecting himself, he exclaimed to those who were around him,

* On part of the ridge of Anti-Lebanon, which looks down upon the city of Damascus, stands a square tower all alone. It reminded me of an expression in the Song of Solomon:—
"Thy nose is as the Tower of Lebanon, which looketh towards Damascus."

and to his fatigued and longing soldiery, "We look but for one Paradise, and that not of this world." He marched on to the capture of Aleppo, and never again beheld the walls of that city, which, like another Capua, might have proved an enervating and demoralizing Elysium of pleasures, whose Circæan spells would infallibly have destroyed the discipline, and relaxed the energy of his enthusiastic and victorious followers.

After gazing for a short space upon the prospect at my feet, I began to descend the road towards the city, and reached the village, or rather town, of Salchié at 5. 40. Here I was much annoyed by the pack of curs which usually infest the streets of all Oriental towns. Poor Ponto was furiously attacked by them, but wearied as he was by his long day's journey, he defended himself most gallantly. We were pursued by the yelping brutes as far as the outer suburbs of Damascus, which we reached at 6. 15. Here I was obliged to take my faithful dog upon my lap, to save him from the fangs of the infuriated curs; I covered him up with my handkerchief to screen him from the view of the Turkish population, to whom even contact with a dog is an abomination, and who are here notorious for their fanaticism and hatred of Christians and Franks.

It is easy to suppose that I was anxious to escape observation and detection, for the Turks permit no Christian to ride through the streets of Damascus, (their holy city) nor to wear a white turban, both of which I was doing, and moreover was carrying my dog upon my knees. I was, however, resolved to run all hazards to preserve the life of my faithful Ponto, and bidding Jiaccomo dismount and walk by my side, and hold the pummel of my saddle, in the Oriental fashion, we passed in safety through bazaars, and gardens, and streets, Jiaccomo answering all questions, by saying that I was a Turk of Stambool, and could not speak Arabic, and that I was on my way to the Pasha. I was wearied to death, and expected every moment to meet with some insult or obstacle to my progress, and had the greatest difficulty in keeping Ponto from betraying his incognito, by his anxious whinings, and attempts to escape from his novel position, and fight his pursuers, many of whom leapt up at him as he lay perdu under the handkerchief, their perceptions being keener than those of the Turks.

Night favouring me, I rode on through gates, and walls, and streets, and reached the gate of the Capuchin convent, in the Christian quarter, at seven o'clock, safe and sound, God be praised for all his mercies, without having met with any accident, or having suffered a moment's illness.

After some delay in getting admittance, the gates being locked, I was ushered into a comfortable apartment, and was cordially received by one of the friars, (Padre Tomaso, a Sardinian.) Here, after bathing my feet in warm water, I supped with the Friar, and went to bed in another room up-stairs at eleven; but, although wearied in mind and body, could get no sleep for bugs, mosquitoes, and fleas, which seemed to be holding a feast and jubilee all night upon my devoted person. It was in vain that I lay down upon my carpet on the floor, for they pursued me even there; indeed the room was literally swarming with vermin.

OCTOBER 16.—My first act this morning was to enter the neat little church of the convent, and there, throwing myself down upon the steps of the principal altar, I returned my humble but fervent thanks to that bountiful Providence who had brought me thus far, alone and unprotected as I was, safe and in good health, to this quiet haven of rest and tranquillity.

After breakfast, I discharged my horses and guide. He attempted (as usual) to extort more money from me than we had bargained for, under the pretence that his master would appropriate to his own use not only the fare of the cattle, but the baakshish of the guide. As I could not be responsible for the honesty of masters towards their servants, I objected to give any thing beyond the arrangement made at Baalbeck, and sent him away much discontented. (I should here observe, that the Orientals always take care to stipulate, beforehand, for a certain bāackshish, or *buona mano*, being given to them upon their completing any job or contract whatever; and as this sum is generally named by themselves, it does not seem fair that they should expect any augmentation afterwards.) *Sono tutti birbanti.*

I made my dragoman, Jiaccomo, a present of a few dollars to buy him a new turban, to his great delight. Indeed, I was so well satisfied with his attention to my interests, and more particularly with his clever conduct with the Emir's people at Baalbeck, that I felt a pleasure in rewarding him.

I occupied myself all this day in purification, and writing up my notes, and a long letter to England, which I forwarded by a Tartar to Constantinople, under cover to Mr. Parish, of the embassy. In the evening I went with Padre Tomaso, to call upon the Friars of the Terra Santa convent. They are Spaniards, and four in number, including the President, Don Manuel de la Valleombrosa. He is a delightful and dignified Castilian. I talked Spanish all the evening as well as I could, but found myself wofully out of practice. The convent is a fine spacious building, and apparently of good revenue. It has under its authority and supervision all the holy places of Syria and Palestine.

OCTOBER 17.—I went to call upon M. Bodin, the French Consular Agent here, and indeed the only Frank functionary in the Holy city of Shem. He was formerly attached to the household of Lady H. Stanhope, in the capacity of dragoman. He is now married to a Christian lady of this place, (an Armenian,) and is well lodged in a beautiful house. He is clothed, and lives in the Oriental style. He related to me some very curious anecdotes of the Pasha Salib. In the afternoon I went to see the bazaars and the merchants' khan.

This is a noble edifice, with six domes, supported by arcades of black and white marble. It has in the centre a large court, full of shady trees, and a fountain: around the court runs a corridor, or gallery, under the arcades; and here are the merchants' stores and magazines.

I regret to say that the plague, which is still raging here, prevents me from examining, as much as I could desire, this interesting city.

While I was at M. Bodin's magazine in the khan, I made an arrangement with the chief Mukrown of a caravan of mules, to provide me with beasts for the journey to Bairout immediately. Bodin recommended my purchasing nothing here but what is absolutely necessary for my journey. He was quite alarmed at observing that I wore a white turban, (which he did not dare to do himself,) and that my papooshes were lined with *green*, the *sacred colour*. He entreated me not to wear them any more, while I staid in Damascus, lest I should expose myself to insult, and even to personal violence.

I observed to him, that the green which I wore in my papooshees could not be the *particular green* which the Mussulmans esteem as sacred, for that surely no Turk would have committed the absurdity of subjecting that colour to the indignity of being trampled upon by any foot; and that, moreover, I had purchased the said papooshes at Smyrna, of a true believer.

He replied, that there was no answering for what caprices the fanatical mob of the city might be guilty of, and that the safest plan was to avoid any circumstance which might give offence. I consented therefore to putting on a pair of red shoes, instead of my yellow papooshes, the more especially, as a friend of mine at Vienna had related to me the history of a great squabble into which he got with these same people of Damascus, for wearing a *white turban;* in which affair he would certainly have lost his life, had it not been for a Turkish Effendi, who came up very opportunely, and saved him from the infuriated mob.

While I was at the khan, M. Bodin introduced me to some of his Turkish friends, most of whom were courteous and good-looking people. He is very much beloved by the Turks, the better class of whom in Damascus (as indeed everywhere else,) are a very amiable and respectable set of men. It is only the *canaille* which is to be dreaded. I had been told that no Frank could dare to walk about the streets of Damascus, unless he were accompanied by a soldier from the Seraglio, to protect him from insult. This is certainly not the case, for I returned from the khan through all the bazaars and most populous parts of the town, merely accompanied by one of the Greek servants of the Capuchin convent. My own man remained at home, fearing the collectors of the *Karatch*, (a poll-tax levied by the Mussulmans upon all their Rayas,) who knowing him for a stranger and an Arab of the mountains, would not have failed to extort money from him. Ponto likewise remained in the convent for fear of his fellow-dogs.

Damascus was once famed as having been the " residence of the Syrian kings; and afterwards, as the regal seat of the Caliphs. Its antiquity is most venerable. It is supposed to have been built by Uz, the son of Abraham, grandson of Shem, the son of Noah, and was the birth-place of Eliezer, the steward of Abraham. It was held by the Mamelukes until 1506, when it was captured by the Turks. Its latitude is 33° 37' north; longitude 37° 4' east. Its famous manufacture of sabres no longer exists. It is, however, still to be found in the Korah Korassan in Persia, whither Tamerlane, at about the beginning of the fifteenth century, forced all the artists in steel to emigrate. The temper of these blades was such as to cut through the finest armour, and to bend from the point to the hilt without breaking." Very fine sabres are to be purchased here at the present moment; but they are either made at Constantinople or in Persia. The principal manufactures are silks, mixed silk and cotton stuffs, velvets, embroidery, soap, saddles, shoes and slippers, tents, cloaks of goat's and camel's hair, and cotton mixed, &c. &c.

The city from without is indeed beautiful; but within, it is like all other Oriental cities, mean and shabby. Its houses are built of mud, and its windows all latticed or turned towards the courts. In rainy weather the streets are running with a muddy mixture, which washes down from the walls of the houses; and in dry weather they are full of dust.

The interior of the houses of the rich is beautiful, full of handsome carpets, divans, inlaid ceilings, gilt cornices, &c.; and the courts are full of fine trees, vines, orange and lemon-plants, and fountains. The groves and gardens which surround the city are indeed beautiful; here, by the side of purling streams and bubbling fountains, the Turks sit in groups, and pass away their days in contemplation, smoking the finest tobacco through amber and jessamine, and drinking the best sherbets and Moka coffee, out of cups of the clearest porcelain. But lovely as are such spots, they teem with danger; for here the pestilence shoots her arrows in silence and rapidity.

The Pashalic of Damascus holds the first rank in Asia, and includes within its limits almost all Palestine and the Holy places. The city is encompassed by a wall, and is watered by three branches of the clear and rapid Barrady. Its population is about two hundred thousand, whereof fifteen thousand are Christians. (Of these latter, I learn from Padre Tomaso, who is a physician, two families are at this moment infected with the plague.)

In my ramble to-day, I observed several people with yellow sticks in their hands. These men were either infected themselves, or were of infected houses. They were all either Greek, Armenian, or Arab Christians. The military force of the city is trifling, consisting of a thousand of the Nizam Djedid (or new victorious army). I am forced to abandon my project of visiting the Pasha, as I understand the Seraglio is full of plague. The principal mosque in the city was once the church of Saint John; it is a fine building, with a handsome dome and minarets. The Turks have a tradition, that at the last day, St. John will descend into this mosque, as they believe Christ will do into that of Omar, (the temple,) at Jerusalem, and Mahomet into that at Mecca. Its gates of brass are very beautiful; but it would cost a Christian his life to set his foot inside of them.

October 18.—M. Bodin sent me one of his friends, a Turkish merchant, to show me some sabres, one of which, a very handsome sword, I purchased for three hundred and eighty piastres. In the afternoon I went with the superior of the Capuchins, Padre Francesco, to see the Lazarite convent. The monks are two in number, Frenchmen, lively fellows, and men of the world. Frenchmen are always so, whether they be laic or cleric. The convent is large and comfortable, and was built by the Jesuits; there is accommodation for about twenty brethren; like every thing that these extraordinary men undertook, it is perfect of its kind, more particularly the church and library. They showed me here, a bible in Hebrew, Chaldean, Syriac, Armenian, Arabic, Greek, and Latin!

In the evening, I called upon Bodin and the friars of the Terra Santa. The president talked a great deal to me about Strangways and Anson, who had passed some time at this convent, previous to their fatal expedition to Aleppo. The fate of poor Anson had excited the sympathy and commiseration of every one in Damascus, Turk as well as Christian. Their amiable qualities, and their determination to face all dangers, and to stand by each other in the hour of peril, had acquired for them the esteem of every body who knew them. They were warned not to go to Aleppo; they were told that the plague was raging all about that country; but they dreaded it not, and paid the forfeit of their perseverance. This evening it rained heavily.

OCTOBER 19.—This morning was cloudy, and comparatively cool. I went in the afternoon to see the house of Ananias, which offers nothing very remarkable. Here are two arched chambers underground, and a little shrine at the upper end, which my Christian conductor kissed with great veneration. I next went out by the eastern gate, through camels and their savage-looking drivers, and proceeded round the walls to the southward, to the gate near which St. Paul was let down in a basket by night. The gate is now walled up, on account of a tradition, that through this entrance the Franks will march into the city.

Hereabouts the walls show some indications of antiquity, and, indeed, nearer to the camel-gate, some relics of the Crusaders, such as a fleur-de-lis, a lion, and a branch of palm and oak. About two furlongs to the left of St. Paul's gate, is the burying-ground of the Christians; and here stands a small altar, inclosed in a kind of wooden cage; this, my guide assured me, was the tomb of St. George; but I believe it to be the place where St. Paul rested on his way to the city, after the vision.

I now returned home, not daring to hire cattle to carry me out to see the place of vision, the lake of meadows, the *cave of Jeremiah, the place of Cain's fratricide, nor the field out of which the Lord took earth, and made Adam therewith.* I could not be sure that the beasts would come from *un luogo pulito*; and the plague is too formidable an antagonist to be sought for. It was my intention to have purchased here two horses for my journey to Cairo, together with saddles, tents, and several articles of fine raiment; but I dreaded lest, with the tent, saddles, and clothing, I might likewise purchase the plague; indeed, both Bodin and the friars dissuaded me as much as possible from making any purchases but of such things as were absolutely indispensable.

OCTOBER 20.—I arose before the sun, and taking a kind leave of my hospitable Capuchins, and making, as is usual, a small present for the use of their church, set off at about six o'clock with two mules, on my return to Bairout. In my passage through the city, I had the greatest difficulty in saving poor Ponto from the savage curs which infest the streets, and which followed us in full cry; indeed, had it not been for Jiaccomo's musket and the long stick of the muleteer, I know not how we should have fared ourselves. At seven I joined a caravan of about

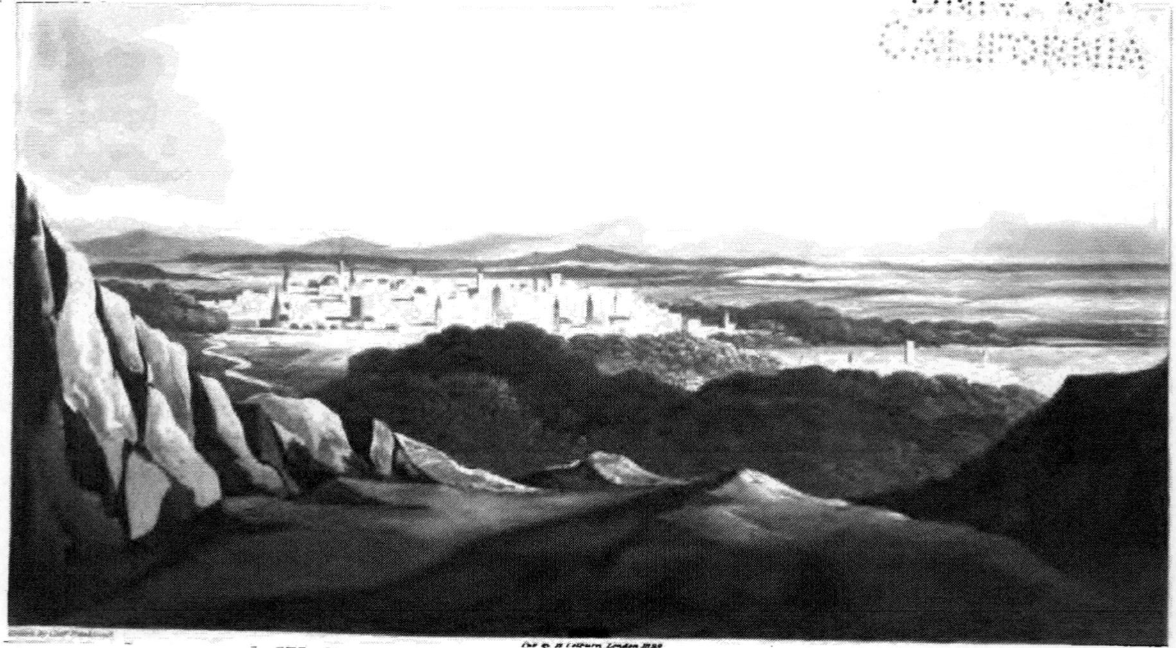

DAMASCUS. 107

forty mules with fourteen drivers. These people were all Christian Arabs of Lebanon, a fine athletic race of men.

We left Damascus by the southern gate, our way leading through gardens of olive, walnut, and pomegranate-trees, and abundance of fig and vine. The morning was deliciously cool, and the air was fragrant with the sweets of a thousand flowers. For about an hour we continued in this kind of scenery, which terminated abruptly at the foot of the dry and calcareous region of Anti-Lebanon. We left the *Khubbe*, which I have before mentioned, on our right hand, and soon began to ascend a volcanic-looking region. I attempted to make a sketch of the Holy City, but it was too much enveloped in fog and smoke to allow of my seeing it clearly. This point of view is not near so advantageous a one as that from near the *Khubbe*.

At ten we were caught in a thunder-storm, and it rained heavily until half-past twelve. We rode on through a low range of mountains, and my mule fell down upon a large sheet of flat stone; but fortunately neither the rider nor the beast suffered any injury. When the rain ceased, we saw some gazelles and many partridges, but could not get near to either. At half-past one, we reached a small Turkish village, called Dimass; and here the muleteers resolved upon halting for the day. I was lodged in an extremely clean cottage, and walked about all the afternoon, examining the remains of an ancient aqueduct, and some other ruins.

OCTOBER 21.—We left Dimass at half-past five in the morning, and passed through the tedious defiles of Anti-Lebanon. As the day dawned, the scenery became more interesting; and at about seven o'clock we approached a very narrow and deep dell, having high limestone rocks on either hand. Here the caravan began to contract its straggling line of march into something of a more compact order, and the muleteers began to fire their muskets.

Upon inquiring why they did so, I was informed, that in this very defile was posted a strong body of Druses, which people were at war with the Christians of Zahle, and had lately plundered a caravan on its way to Damascus, and killed some of its muleteers; that they fired off their muskets in order to show the Druses that they were well armed and prepared for resistance. I next inquired what plan the chief of the caravan had to propose in case he should find the pass occupied by the Druses. He replied, that they should go quietly on until they reached the pass, and that then they should be hailed by the Druses, and desired to pay down a certain sum of money as a tribute; upon which they would be suffered to pass. I asked him, if it were his intention to pay this money in the event of it being demanded of him. He replied, with indignation, No! that they were fourteen in number, and were people of courage, and would resist the demand, and force their way through.

Finding that our Capo was so resolute, I thought it best to endeavour to methodize his line of march a little, and to put ourselves into a better posture for defence. I proposed to him to order forward two of his most resolute men to feel the way for us, and to give notice, by firing their pistols, of any danger. I represented to him, that by going all in one body, we might be drawn into the pass, and find ourselves surrounded by the Druses before we were at all aware of our danger. He replied, that he could not order any body to quit their mules, and that indeed he did not think that any two of them would like to try the pass, unsupported by the rest. Among the muleteers there was a venerable old Arab, with a long white beard, the father of our Capo, and several others of the party. He came up, and said that the Frangi had spoken good words; but that he did not think any body would undertake the task of *eclaireur*, unless the Frangi himself were the man.

Upon interrogating Jiaccomo, (who had once been a soldier, and had fought several battles for the Emir Beshir against the Sheik Beshir,) and finding that he was disposed to accompany me, we examined the state of our arms, and set off upon our stupid and unwarlike mules at a trot, and gaining about three hundred yards upon the convoy, began to examine cautiously the different rocks, bushes, and patches of brushwood which lay before us. I own I had not much confidence in the courage of the mule-drivers, and expected, in case of an attack, that they would abandon both the cargoes of the mules, myself and man, to the Druses, and take care of their own personal safety by flight. Fortunately for us all, there was nobody in the pass; and I had the satisfaction of seeing the whole caravan debouche into the plain of the Bakaa at about noon. We had now a fine view of the ranges of Mount Lebanon, particularly Gebbail Sennin in our front.

We passed the villages of el Margi and Argi, on our left and right hands. In the former are some ancient remains, principally a large square tower of Cyclopean construction, standing upon a hill above the village; probably this has been a fortress: doubtlessly the plain of the Bakaa was once much peopled and full of towns, its fine rich loam and its advantageous situation affording so fair a field for cultivation and population; but wherever the proud sons of Othman have trod, they have left behind them a trace like that made by a flight of locusts; all withers and perishes beneath their fatal touch!

At 1. 30. we reached and crossed Nahr el Anjoul, (the river of the Angel,) and arrived at Khan el Margi at two o'clock. Here, to our great discomfiture we found a caravan, of four hundred camels from Damascus, going to the coast with kali, to fetch back corn which had been sent by the Grand Signor by sea to Bairout, for the use of the pashalic of Damascus. The grouping of these huge unwieldy beasts, and their drivers occupied in unloading them, was highly picturesque and Oriental.

The situation of the Khan is beautiful: in its front is the lofty range of Lebanon; in its rear, the less rugged and less lofty chain of Anti-Lebanon; to the right and left, the immense plain of the Bakaa, extending itself between the parallel lines of mountains as far as the eye can reach; Baalbeck, with its woods of walnuts, distantly seen on the right; the villages of Abelias and Mar Abelias on the right and left front, at the foot of Lebanon, and Argi and Margi at that of Anti-Lebanon. Close to the khan runs a muddy and a sleepy river, along whose banks I strolled with my gun, hoping to get near some wild ducks and some grey-spotted kingfishers which I saw, but could not get a shot at. The khan itself is a large quadrangular building of mud, having in its interior a kind of double corridor, underneath which we reposed upon clean mats in the inner, and the mules ate their chaff in the outer. My neighbours were two Turkish merchants from Aleppo,—I was very civil to them, and gave them coffee and arrack. The muleteers and camel-drivers made a great noise all night, and the fleas, as usual, prevented my sleeping much.

OCTOBER 22.—I arose at daylight, but found that the muleteers had all gone to attend the funeral of one of their brethren in the village of Margi. He had died, it seemed, rather sudto allow time for the caravan of mules to overtake me. I alighted near a little cottage, and from thence had a beautiful prospect of Mar Mousa, Cornail, and many other villages. At our feet was a kind of deep punch-bowl, full of vines, figs, and cultivation.

After an hour's repose, the convoy having joined, we set off again, passing over a most execrable road. The face of the earth hereabouts is covered with an iron-looking stone or scoria, very much honeycombed, and looking as if it had passed through a smelting house. Sometimes there were whole beds of it covering a substratum of limestone. (This is evidently a posterior formation. Query, is it volcanic?) At half-past four we reached Khan el Lassan, very much fatigued, as well as my mules, one of whom fell repeatedly. Here we found the plague, and were obliged to bivouack in a mulberry-garden, at a little distance from the village and khan.

While I was reposing at the foot of my mulberry-tree, I received a visit from the Sheik of that district. He was a handsome, well-dressed fellow, and was accompanied by his secretary and chäoush. As they all came from an infected place, I was obliged to keep them at a very respectful distance, but treated them, as well as the two Aleppo merchants who were near me, to coffee and arrack. The merchants began to open their packs, and expose their fine gold and silver stuffs, cloaks of camel's hair, turbans, and shawls, &c. &c. for sale. I was much amused with the mutual attempts made by the Sheik and themselves, to out-manœuvre each other in their bargains. The Sheik, however, was a rich fellow, *(un principe Emir,)* and purchased several stuffs, paying, however, about one half of what the Turks demanded in the first instance. He was very curious about my arms, knife, and watch, and wished very much to purchase every thing that I had of European manufacture, more particularly my pen-knife, which had four blades, one of which was for cutting the nails, which operation he performed with infinite satisfaction. He would not however accept it as a present, and I could not allow him to purchase it. At nightfall he took his leave, with many expressions of regard and offers of service.

One of the Aleppo merchants was a Hadjee, and wore a large green turban; he was a morose-looking, and, I thought, rather an uncivil fellow.

I could not help thinking of the Arab proverb, which I had frequently heard repeated: "If thy neighbour has made the pilgrimage to Mecca once, distrust him; if twice, beware of him; if thrice, get thee away in haste from his neighbourhood."

After they had sold some of their goods to the Sheik, I was desirous of purchasing a turban of Aleppo manufacture from them, at a reasonable price; they made great professions of regard for me, as they had received civilities at my hands on the route, and said, that for the sake of our companionship, they would make me a present of it, or of any thing else I might choose to select out of their bales, upon our arrival at Bairout.

However, I never saw any more either of them or of their goods, their recollection of me failing when *they no longer drank my coffee and arrack.*

The Sheik had not been gone long, when the caravan of camels came up, and passed by our bivouack. These beasts, by their horrid groanings and discordant bellowings, kept me awake all night long.

OCTOBER 23.—We broke up our bivouack before the dawn; but ere I set off, the owner of the mulberry-garden came to ask for a baackshish, for the inestimable privilege I had enjoyed of sleeping under one of his trees. These people ask money for every thing. I of course refused to give him a para. He observed, that all the Frangi who had ever passed that way had paid him for occupying the ground; but I have been paying for being a stranger too long, to suffer myself to be any longer gulled by every person who chooses to make a demand upon my purse.

Our road was one of the worst I have ever yet seen; and as it was not yet day, it was extremely dangerous, being full of large loose stones, and of very rapid descent. I was often obliged to get off my mule and pick my way on foot. It is part of the policy of the Emir Beshir, to keep the mountain roads nearly impracticable; and by this means he adds to the security of his dominions, more than he could do by the maintenance of a large armed force. The most formidable arm of the Turks, is their cavalry, and to them this mountain region is almost inaccessible. Nay, I am informed that this crafty Prince often causes the roads to be made worse, in the neighbourhood of the Turkish Pashas; and this I can very easily believe to be the case.

As the day dawned, we had a fine view of the sea, the plains and sands of Bairout, and of the mountainets crowned with convents and villages. At seven we passed near the bed of the river Berytus, and its ancient aqueduct, (which I have mentioned in page 362, vol. i.) to our right hand, but did not see this structure, it lying too far down beneath us, and being hidden by the projecting promontories. Far up above us on our right, was also the convent of Deir el Kalaā, where I had passed so many days under my tent. At half-past eight we reached the pines and plains of Bairout, and at ten, the Consular house, *fuor le mura*. The Consul and his daughter had come down on the preceding evening, from Deir el Kalaā, and they were still in bed. I did not like to disturb their slumbers, so rode on into the town of Bairout, and here, to my great surprise as well as pleasure, I found Mr. Strangways; who, after being shut up seven months in Aleppo, where he had the grief to see his dear friend Anson die, had just returned here by Tripoli, where he had been passing some weeks with the fine gallant old Pasha, (the surviving relic of the Mamelukes,) and is now on his way to Cairo. He travels *en Grand Seigneur*, with five horses, one of which is a present from the worthy Pasha, and has his dragoman, (a fine youth of Aleppo,) and three servants. In the afternoon I called upon Mr. Abbott, and dined with Strangways and St. John, at six o'clock, at the Locanda Inglese, a very good inn kept by a Maltese.

NOTES AND INSCRIPTIONS.

I know not what the traveller in Syria would do were it not for the Frank convents, which, like so many Oases in the Desert, are scattered about this country. They are become the deposits of the Christian virtues, and are so many rallying points of civilization. I owe them this slight tribute of gratitude.

Found upon a broken entablature at Facra.—See page 32.

ΟΙΗΝΤΡΑϹΕΙΙΟΙ

Upon the corner-stone in the north front of the supposed Mausoleum of Facra.—See p. 32.

ΣΕΝΤΕΠΙϹΟΛΟΜ.....
ΡΑΒΒΟΜΟΥΕΗΜΕ.....
ΑΗΤΟΥΕΚΤΜΤΟΥ
ΜΕΤΙΣΤΟΥΟΕΟΥUΚΟΛΟ
ΜΗΟΗ

N. B. The dotted lines signify illegible.

NOTES AND INSCRIPTIONS.

Upon a broken entablature in the south wall at Baalbeck, inverted.—See page 69.

TPARXOYKΛIΛYΓ
ANEAHKEN

Upon a stone in the wall of the water-mill, opposite to the village of El Souk.—See page 88.

CTOYCHZYXYCTPOYΛΔIIUCCY.......
HICYWHKIOHOACIIHTWKYPICD
YΠeCeCUTHPIACKYHOY \
KAICAPOCAYCIACKAICΠOY
HOCKAIANCI:ΠOYIOHYCA
OKCCHIHΔKbNIOK:COUON
ANCΘHKAKIKAIΠAIOΔICOAO
CIANeΠOHCAN

N. B. The dotted line signifies erased and illegible.

As I am, unfortunately for me, no Grecian, I must leave the deciphering of these mutilated inscriptions to the scholar; answering for nothing but the correctness of the copyist, who did all he could to make exact fac-similes of them. It appears, however, to me, that this is the same character with that of the inscriptions which I copied in the plains of Troy, which are generally allowed to be of the Byzantine age. These remains, then, cannot be of any very remote antiquity.

ANECDOTE OF PASHA SALIB, OF DAMASCUS.

One morning, during my short stay in the city of Shem, I was very much surprised by the apparition of a visitor, clad in Frank attire; a circumstance until now unknown in Damascus. This person informed me, that he had come here to cast cannon for the Pasha; that he was a Smyrniot Frenchman, and had been in the service of the Greeks under Favier; but that, like almost all the Philhellene adventurers, he had been disgusted with them, and had quitted their service for one which he looked upon as being more likely to appreciate and to reward his merits. He remained some time with me; but I could not divine what was the motive of his visit. I gathered from him, however, that he was not very well satisfied with his present situation, and that he intended shortly to return to Bairout, and so find his way back to Smyrna, by way of Cyprus and Milo.

In the afternoon I called upon Bodin, the French Consular Agent, and from him I learned, that although the Pasha had held out great hopes to the Philhellene, and had promised to set him to work immediately in casting cannon; yet that his Excellency was too parsimonious to lay out the necessary money in the purchase of metal and the construction of founderies; and that when he found that the Smyrniot could not make guns without the aid of the above-mentioned costly articles, his ardour for the service of his Highness the Sultan, and the equipment of his corps of artillerists, (topchis,) degenerated into civil speeches to the Philhellene, and excuses for delay. Meanwhile, the luckless Smyrniot was starving for want of a few piastres to pay his daily expenses; and he in vain entreated the Pasha to advance him a small sum upon his promised appointments, to support his wife and children, who had accompanied him from Bairout hither.

The Pasha, who was anxious to rid himself of the cannon founderer, and of his importunities, was determined to advance him nothing more than was sufficient to keep soul and body together, well foreseeing that the unfortunate dupe would, by such means, be compelled either to quit the country or to starve; either of which alternatives was equally agreeable to his Excellency. It fell out as he had foreseen; for the poor devil was obliged at length to apply for permission to return to Bairout, and for a small sum to pay his expenses thither.

While he was at the seraglio, soliciting this great favour of the Pasha, M. Bodin arrived upon a somewhat similar errand. He had been in the habit of advancing large sums of money to the Pasha, and had come with the intention of withdrawing from the reluctant Turk ten thousand piastres (about one hundred and sixty-six pounds sterling.)

Upon his making his appearance, the Pasha immediately seized upon so favourable an occasion for ridding himself of the Philhellene and his claims at the same time. His Excellency expressed great delight at seeing Bodin, the more particularly, as he said he had come just in time to render assistance to his needy countryman, who, being a French subject, had a right to claim his aid. He observed, that Bodin was the proper person to whom the Philhellene should have applied for relief; and begged that the Consular Agent would forthwith advance him four hundred piastres to pay his journey to Bairout. "But," said M. Bodin, "I am come with the intention of begging of your Excellency ten thousand piastres, which you owe me, and of which I stand in the greatest need. I protest to you, that I have not a piastre in my compting-house, and know not from whence to procure these four hundred which you desire me to pay this man."

—" Never mind," said the Pasha; " you can borrow them of some of your friends; it will only make me so much the more your debtor. It is not worth my while to give an order upon my seraff (banker) for so small a sum; and I have just sent off the last para from my treasury to the Porte. You have now an opportunity of adding to my obligations towards you, of which I am very sensible, and at the same time of relieving a distressed countryman. As for your ten thousand piastres, depend upon my justice and the Mussulman good faith, for their being repaid to you some day with interest, and leave me, for the present, to the avocations and important functions of my government."— Thus, by dint of artifice and effrontery, the Pasha rid himself of two claimants at a time.

CHAPTER III.

Strangways sets off for Cairo. — A Greek squadron comes into the port of Bairout. — I set off for Jerusalem. — Khan Bourghaldi.—Tombs.—Djissir Damoor.—Ancient remains.—Nabyoonas, the place of Jonah's miraculous disembarkation.—View of Saide.—Khan el Aoule.—Visit to Lady Hester Stanhope at Djouni.—Saide, or Sidon.— Intelligence of the Battle of Navarino reaches us.—Embarrassments.—Generous offer of protection from a Metooali Chief.—I abandon my projected journey to Jerusalem for the present. — Anecdote of Sultan Mahmoud and Mehmet Ali Pasha.—I leave Djouni for the Palace of the Emir Beshir (Prince of the Druses).—Reception from the Emir.—M. Aubin's account of Navarino, and advice how to proceed.—Plague at Deir el Kamaār.— Abdha.—Arrival at Shia, near Bairout.—Maronite curate, his daughter, and hospitality.—Arrival at Mansouree.— I go to Deir el Kalaā.—I am attacked by the fever of the country.—Return to the neighbourhood of Bairout.—Projects for departure to Alexandria. — His Majesty's ship Pelorus arrives.—I embark in her for Cyprus and Alexandria.—Miscellaneous remarks on Syria.

October 24.—I received a visit from Strangways and Chasseaud, and was occupied with my tailor and journals all the forenoon.

October 27.—A Greek brig is off the port; great alarm prevails in the city; the Pasha's schooner has hauled down her colours.

October 28.—Strangways left us for Cairo. I was employed in looking for horses to purchase, for my journey into Egypt, but without success.

October 29.—Thunder storms and heavy rain.

October 30.—Ditto, ditto.

October 31.—Three Greek brigs and a chatouille came into the port, and were cannonaded by the castles, in despite of which they visited a French brig lying in the roads, within half-gun-shot of the forts; but she being empty, they found her not worth fighting about. The Greeks came in under Turkish colours, and under them sustained the cannonade without returning a shot; but when their boat had returned from visiting the Frenchman, they hoisted Greek ensigns and pennants, and the Commodore fired one gun, in token of contempt, at the Pasha's schooner, which had come close in under the castle walls. I was disappointed in not seeing them take the schooner off. I sat all the while upon the flat roof of the Consular house, underneath the flag-staff, watching the scene and enjoying extremely the bustle and activity of the armed population; the Turks running about, shouting, and roaring, the Arnäouts thronging into the old dilapidated castles, and the fine old Mootselim (a Georgian) sitting tranquilly smoking his pipe near a great long gun, giving his directions as quietly as if he were on his divan.

Bairout is defended upon the shore by *three* guns only, one of which has lost its muzzle, and the others are not in the best possible state. There are a few other pieces of artillery, mounted upon a high square tower, about eight hundred yards from the sea; but I suspect their condition is not very formidable. Some few months ago, a division of Greek brigs landed a body of men, after cannonading the town; these attempted to scale the walls, and very nearly succeeded in their enterprise, but were driven back by a few resolute Turks, who, from the tower of a mosque, killed about half a dozen of them.

The Emir Beshir came down with about four thousand men from the mountain, to the pines, but remained a tranquil spectator of the affair. The Greeks seemed to have no leader, and returned to their vessels without effecting any thing; perhaps they expected to have been assisted by the town's people of the Christian communion. This affair served, however, as a pretext to Abdullah Pasha for ill treating the unfortunate Greek and Arab inhabitants, from whom he extorted large sums of money. His Delhis and Hawaree Arabs attacked likewise the houses of the Franks, and especially of the American missionaries.

November 1.—I made preparations for departure, but could procure no beasts without paying an extravagant price for them. At night, two vessels stood into the roads, supposed to be Greeks; great panic prevailed in the town, and an immense shouting was made all night by the watchmen. Indeed the noise made by them every night, the buzzing of mosquitoes, the biting of fleas, and the barking of dogs, keep me from sleeping.

NOVEMBER 2.—I engaged two mules, to start to-morrow at daybreak for Saide, at six piastres a-head. I took leave of Chasseaud and St. John, and paid an extravagant bill at the Locanda Inglese.

NOVEMBER 3.—Upon rising in the morning, I found that the muleteer had decamped, having made another bargain with some one else. The whole day was spent in vain attempts to procure animals. I dined at Chasseaud's, and towards evening, by help of his servant, made a bargain with a Turkish muckrow, to secure whose fidelity, I took from him some money as a pledge.

NOVEMBER 4.—I left Bairout at 7. 30. in the morning. I passed the pines at 8. 15., and was much struck with the extreme beauty of the spot. I must confess that they are infinitely more beautiful than the *celebrated cedars*. The road led through a deep red sand. Cactus, and olives, and Oriental sycamores adorn the hedges. I saw many tortoises drop into the pools of stagnant water as I passed by, giving them the alarm. The sea was on our right hand, and the mountains, with their picturesque Arab towns and vineyards, on our left. Camels and Arabs, beach and fishing-boats, completed the scene.

At eleven, I reached a number of old tombs of the same description with those at Deir el Kalaā; many of them seemed to be still unopened. The limestone mountain on our left hand seemed to be full of them. At 11. 15. I reached Khan Bourghaldi; here I breakfasted. I inquired about the tombs; and was told that they were supposed to be Hebrew, and that there were some excavated in the sides of the rocks, (like unto that one which I saw at Facra,) one of which has a Hebrew inscription. I inquired for coins, but without success. In front of Khan Bourghaldi is an old ruined square tower, probably of Crusade origin. At 12. 30. I left the khan, and proceeded along the beach, the sand being there rendered firm by the water. The day was exceedingly hot.

At 2. 30. I reached Djissir Damoor; a bridge broken down by the force of the winter's torrents. Here was plenty of olianders and high reeds. I had a fine view through a deep ravine into the mountains. At three I reached part of a Roman road and an old tower. At 3. 30. I found the remains of a large city on my left hand. (Query, ancient Sidon?) At four I reached Nabyoonas, the place of Jonah's disembarkation from the whale. The Turks, who " believe and tremble," have here built two little mosques, and here is likewise a khan. At sunset, having just doubled a point, I obtained a fine view of Saide and its little port, a brig (said to be Greek) was lying there; I observed a salute fired. *C'est la fête St. Charles.* The road was stony and rocky in the extreme; then sand and beach, then rock again. At 6. 40. I entered groves of olive and vines. At seven, I reached Khan Djissir el Aoule; ere I bivouacked under a mulberry-tree, and wrote a letter, by moonlight, to Lady Hester Stanhope at Djouni, about three hours by the horse-road from hence in the mountain.

NOVEMBER 5.—I arose at five by the light of a splendid moon, (a little past the full,) and despatched a messenger to Lady H. Stanhope with my letter, he promising to return in two hours and a half. I waited for him until noon, when suspecting either that some accident had happened to him, or that her Ladyship was absent, I resolved to set out for Saide, and had actually commenced my route, when the messenger returned *(punica fides)* with a note from her Ladyship, requesting me to come immediately and see her, she sending at the same time one of her servants to conduct me. The messenger, who had been absent seven hours instead of two and a half, insisted, however, upon being paid as if he had performed his contract, which was, that if he did not return with an answer in the given time, he was only to receive half of his fare, unless the answer assigned some good cause for his delay. I gave him one piastre and half.

Her Ladyship's servant told me however, afterwards, the reason of the delay. The messenger had a bullock to drive back from the mountain, and this he knew ere he set out, well knowing that he could never have performed the task in the given time, but trusting to my carelessness and his own impudence to help him out.

I reached Djouni at 3. 15. It is seated upon a conical hill, surrounded by mountains and deep dells. Her Ladyship has built a wall all around it, to keep out the jackals, hyenas, and bears. I was ushered by her janissaries and chäoüx into a pretty little pavilion in the gardens, where I found all sorts of English comforts and luxuries, from which I had been now so long estranged, that I felt quite delighted upon beholding them.

About five o'clock I was conducted to her Ladyship's presence. She was dressed *à l'Arabe*, and is a very imposing and noble-looking personage, of great height, and dignified manners. She received me very graciously, and we soon became acquainted with each other. I dined alone, she never eating after one o'clock.

After dinner I again returned to her Ladyship, and remained *tête-à-tête* with her until midnight, much entertained and instructed by her conversation, which is lively and interesting, extraordinary and impressive by turns.

NOVEMBER 6.—I enjoyed a nice, clean, English-feeling bed until eight o'clock. One leaves one's carpet with no regret; but a soft clean bed has irresistible attractions. In the afternoon I walked with her Ladyship round her pretty gardens. She has laid out large sums of money upon this place, and has indeed contrived to make a little paradise in the desert. *Tête-à-tête* until midnight.

NOVEMBER 7.—In the morning I rode into Saide, (distant about three or four hours,) to purchase horses, Lady Hester having been so kind as to send into the town yesterday one of her servants to look out for such horses as were for sale. In my way I passed by the Khan el Aoule, getting well drenched by a heavy shower; and proceeded along the beach, towards the picturesque and castellated city.

I believe that it possesses no remains of antiquity of earlier date than the Crusades. The Christians lost it in the beginning of the twelfth century; it was however retaken in 1250, by St. Louis, who repaired its fortifications. It again fell into the hands of the Saracens in 1289, when the famous Emir Fakreddin destroyed the harbour, by sinking in it many columns of stone, lest the Franks (or, perhaps, the Turks,) should again wrest it from his hands. I observed in one of the gates part of a Gothic alto relievo, a dog seizing a stag.

I went to the French khan, and was well received by her Ladyship's agent, an old Frenchman, with an Arab dress and cocked hat. I saw some very beautiful horses, belonging to an Aga of Arnäouts, and the Mootselim; these dignitaries receiving me politely, and showing off their cattle.

They were too high-priced, too high-fed, and

too high-mettled for my purpose:—the price being from three to four purses, (1,500 or 2,000 piastres.) At length, after some difficulty, I succeeded in finding a pretty little brown horse, and a gedishe, (gelding,) the former for my own riding, and the latter for my servant and baggage. The geldings of this country are all taught to amble, and are good beasts for my purpose. I returned to Djouni at about five. *Tête-à-tête* until past midnight.

I wish I could prevail upon Lady Hester to write her memoirs. She has seen more of the world, both civilized and barbarous, than any body in existence, and has all the talent necessary to write an excellent book. It rained all night.

NOVEMBER 8.—The morning deliciously cool. In the afternoon, a letter came from the French Consul at Saide to her Ladyship, announcing the arrival of a French man-of-war at Bairout from Alexandria, bringing the intelligence of the almost total destruction of the Turco-Egyptian fleet at Navarino by the combined squadrons.—The Franks have all fled to the mountain, both at Bairout and Saide. We know not what to think of so extraordinary and unlooked-for a piece of intelligence. For my part, I do not credit it, but think it is most likely an exaggeration of some misunderstanding between the Christian and Infidel commanders. Meanwhile, I am, to be sure, most fortunate in being, at such an alarming moment, under the roof of a person so highly respected and esteemed by the Turks, as Lady Hester Stanhope.

November 9.—I rode, after breakfast, to Djouni, charged with a communication to a French family, who had very unceremoniously taken possession of a house of Lady Hester's at that place. Here I saw the French Consul of Bairout's letter, and could not make out the news to be official. This evening, I was attacked by a slight fever, accompanied by a sore throat. I went to bed, and fasted. Lady Hester's kindness and solicitude were delightful. I bathed my feet in hot water, drank barley water and syrup of violets, and in the course of the night contrived to perspire profusely.

Lady Hester has given me one of her own servants to accompany me as a sieys (groom), a Turk.

NOVEMBER 10.—This morning I am nearly free from fever; the perspiration profuse; but the sore throat rather ulcerated; I gargle with Eau de Cologne and water; my head-ache is abated. In the evening, *tête-à-tête* as usual with her Ladyship. I consulted with her as to the best mode of proceeding. I fear I must totally abandon all hopes of continuing my tour. After I had retired to my bed-room, information reached her Ladyship that a Russian and a French man-of-war had arrived at Acre, and demanded their Consul at that place, whom it would seem the Pasha had refused to give up to them. All this looks as if hostilities either had or were likely to commence.

I am not the only guest at Djouni. Lady Hester informs me, that she has at this moment two great Mahometan visitors under her roof, although I never see them by any accident.

One of these is a Mollah, learned in the law of the Prophet; and the other is a Metooali chief, from the Bakaa, near Baalbeck. These men are aware that I am here, and asked her Ladyship about me; but she, wishing to evade the subject, said I was a Georgian.

November 11.—The morning is delightfully fine. I think of falling back towards Bairout, or rather to the mountains thereabouts, in order to be in the way of embarking in case any vessel-of-war should touch there. I do not wish to embarrass Lady Hester, by claiming the protection of her roof in such a delicate conjuncture; for although she seems determined to remain in this country under all circumstances, and that she has sufficient influence with the Turks to enable her so to do, still it would be putting her complaisance and theirs to rather a severe test, should I and other Franks choose to throw ourselves, with all our difficulties, upon her shoulders; for she has no other rights or privileges in this country than those which Oriental hospitality, and the indulgence of the Turkish Government towards her person, accord. To-morrow, therefore, I must run the gauntlet through the Turks towards Antoura, where I think I may await in safety some opportunity to embark for Greece and Malta. So then, adieu to all my projects of visiting the interesting scenes of the Holy Land, when I am upon its threshold; and adieu to Egypt, which I had hoped to have reached ere another month had passed over my head.

This morning the Metooali chief set off for his own country; but before he went, he told Lady Hester, that he was perfectly aware that she was, at the present moment, giving the shelter of her house to a countryman of her own. "But," said he, " it is possible that the Pasha of Acre may oblige you to surrender him up. Now, if he will confide himself to my care, I will carry him away into the Bakaa among my own people. I do not fear the Pashas of Acre or Damascus; and as I am in constant communication with the coast, I shall know whenever a Frank vessel touches either at Tripoli or Bairout, and I will answer with my life for his. . Will your countryman trust a Metooali ?"

Lady Hester mentioned this circumstance to me, and left it open to me to accept the proposal of her friend. I had so little apprehension of any danger, that I declined availing myself of this generous offer of protection for the present; always reserving to myself the power of opening a communication upon the subject with the Metooali Chief, through Lady Hester, upon any future emergency.

At midnight I took leave of Lady Hester Stanhope.

Among the many interesting conversations which I have had with Lady Hester, she related several anecdotes of the people of the East, most of which were extremely illustrative of their manners and superstitions.

I select the following, as it relates to the two greatest men of which the East can boast— Sultan Mahmoud, and Mehmet Ali.

The growing power of the Pasha of Egypt

had long been the cause of uneasiness to the Sublime Porte. It was feared, at Stambool, that Mehmet Ali would some day throw off the yoke of the successor to the Caliphat.

In vain the perfidious policy of the Seraglio despatched Capidgi Bashis, armed with the bowstring and the dagger, to the capital of the Pyramids; in vain its treacherous agents endeavoured, by poison or by stratagem, to rid the Porte of a dangerous rival. Mehmet Ali was too well warned by his spies at Constantinople, of the toils which were spread around him, to suffer himself to fall into the snare.

At length the Sultan Mahmoud resolved upon adopting a scheme, which should be so cleverly devised, and involved in such impenetrable secrecy, that it was impossible it could fail of success.

He had in the Imperial Harem a beautiful Georgian slave, whose innocence and beauty fitted her, in the Sultan's eyes, for the atrocious act of perfidy of which she was to be the unsuspecting agent.

The belief in talismans is still prevalent throughout the East; and perhaps even the enlightened Mahmoud himself is not superior to the rest of his nation in matters of traditionary superstition.

He sent one day for the fair Georgian, and affecting a great love for her person, and desire to advance her interests, told her, that it was his imperial will to send her to Egypt, as a present to Mehmet Ali, whose power and riches were as unbounded as the regions over which he held the sway of a sovereign Prince, second to no one in the universe but to himself, the great Padisha.

He observed to her, how much happiness would fall to her lot, if she could contrive to captivate the affections of the master for whom he designed her; that she would become, as it were, the Queen of Egypt, and would reign over boundless empires.

But, in order to insure to her so desirable a consummation of his imperial wishes for her welfare and happiness, he would present her with a talisman, which he then placed upon her finger. " Watch," said he, " a favourable moment, when the Pasha is lying on your bosom, to drop this ring into a glass of water; which, when he shall have drunk, will give you the full possession of his affections, and render him your captive for ever.

The unsuspecting Georgian eagerly accepted the lot which was offered to her, and, dazzled by its promised splendour, determined upon following the instructions of the Sultan to the very letter.

In the due course of time she arrived at Cairo, with a splendid suite, and many slaves, bearing rich presents.

Mehmet Ali's spies had, however, contrived to put him on his guard. Such a splendid demonstration of esteem from his Imperial Master alarmed him for his safety.

He would not suffer the fair Georgian to see the light of his countenance; but after some detention in Cairo, made a present of her to his *intimate friend*, Billel Aga, the Governor of

Alexandria, of whom, by the bye, the Pasha had long been jealous.

The poor Georgian having lost a Pasha, thought she must do her best to captivate her Aga, and administered to him the fatal draught, in the manner Sultan Mahmoud had designed for Mehmet Ali. The Aga fell dead upon the floor. The Georgian shrieked and clapped her hands: in rushed the eunuchs of the harem, and bore out the dead body of their master.

When the Georgian was accused of poisoning the Aga, she calmly denied the fact. " What did you do to him?" was the question. " I gave him a glass of water, into which I had dropped a talisman. See, there is the glass, and there is the ring."

The ring, it was true, remained; but the *stone*, which it had encircled, was *melted in the water*.

NOVEMBER 12.—At half-past nine I set off for the Palace of the Emir Beshir, with the intention of learning from him what chance of protection in his dominions existed for us under the present circumstances. I rode through an uninteresting and steep mountain country all the day, arriving at Teddin, his Highness's residence, at four in the evening. It is a large straggling building of hewn stone, but without any particular beauty or character. Here I found a quarantine established, and sent in my name, and the nature of my business, to the Emir by a capidgee.

I waited outside about an hour, without obtaining any answer to my message. At length a certain Signor Francesco made his appearance, a fat, piggish-looking Italian doctor, who, after hearing the nature of my business, answered phlegmatically enough, that they were all in quarantine, and that the Emir was now ill and asleep; but that if I wished it, he would speak to the Emir for me. I replied, that I came to ask no favour from the Emir, but that I merely wanted a place to put my head in, and to be informed where I should go, in order to be out of the way of the Turks for the present; that I did not expect the Emir would have shut the door in my face in this manner; but that I could sleep under a tree, as I had hitherto done, and would set off in the morning, to rejoin the Consul of my nation, without being under an obligation to any body.

Upon this I withdrew to the mountain side, and took up my bivouack under a tree. I had not, however, remained there long, ere the Emir (having, no doubt, heard from Signor Francesco all that had passed between us,) sent his secretary to me, to say that he was sorry that he could not see me himself; that such was the delicate posture of affairs, that he feared to give umbrage to the Turks; but that out of respect to my nation and to Lady Hester Stanhope, he would certainly give me an asylum, and that there was a room prepared for me. Upon this, I marched down in great form to the palace, and was shown into a large dirty room upon the ground-floor, in a kind of stable-yard. Here, however, I spread my carpets and made myself comfortable. The Emir sent me coffee and supper, &c. &c., and his principal physician, M. Aubin, to compliment me.

From this gentleman I learnt all the particulars of the battle of Navarino (he, of course, giving all the credit to the French). He recommended my going on in the morning to Antoura, there to await the course of events. He remarked, that the Emir could not openly protect the Franks, but that the mountain was vast and inaccessible to the Turks; that we might trust to the magnanimity and good heart of the Emir, &c. &c. &c. All this I looked upon as a kind of semi-official communication, and therefore determined upon setting out in the morning for the mountain, near Bairout. It rained all night.

November 13.—I set off about seven. The plague was at Deir el Kamaar.* All the sick people came to the mill for flour, by a route apart. I passed by many charnel houses, and inhaled the odour thereof. I avoided the town, going by a road beneath it, and passing through

* Deir el Kamaar is the capital city of the Druses.

fine rocky scenery, at eleven, I reached Nahr el Damaar; the bed of the river is through a solid mass of calcareous rock; here is a neat bridge of two arches. I found the ascent on the opposite side tedious and steep. An abandoned coal mine is on the left hand. I had a view of the sea, and Bairout, at two. At three, I reach Abdha, where I expected to find the French; the birds were all flown, with the exception of Madame Guys, the Consul's wife, and her children. I had an interview with an impertinent dragoman, who pretended to be very mysterious and diplomatic respecting the place of refuge (perhaps he took me for a spy). I dined under a tree, and arrived at Shia, near the pines of Bairout, at sunset. I went to the Maronite curate's, (an uncle of my servant's,) and found a clean house, and hospitable reception and treatment. The curate had a pretty daughter, well dressed in the costume of an Arab lady. I wrote to Mr. Abbott at Deir el Kalaa. I supped with the curate, and servants, and muleteer. Here I found no fleas, a clean bed, and sound sleep.

November 14.—I received a note from Mr. Abbott, recommending my going up to Mansouree, where he had just taken a good house. I set off about nine, and reached Mansouree at eleven; here I found Mr. and Mrs. Godell, the American missionaries, Mr. and Mrs. Abbott, and Mr. St. John. The Consul showed me the official account of the battle, in which it would seem that the English had borne the principal part, as their loss is the heaviest. Eighty of the Turco-Egyptian fleet have been either totally destroyed, or put quite out of the possibility of ever going to sea again. It appears that the fight took place on account of the Turks having fired into a boat of His Majesty's ship Dartmouth, and killed an officer and five men; their death has been well avenged by that of five or six thousand Turks and Egyptians!!! There are three merchant vessels lying in the eastern harbour of Bairout; shall I go away in one of them for Europe? or shall I await the news from Constantinople, and still adhere to my plan of seeing Egypt, going thither by sea? In the afternoon, the Consul, his wife, and Mr. St. John, returned to Deir el Kalaa, and we dined at the house of one of the *converts*, a young Greek Deacon, with a pretty Arab wife and child.

NOVEMBER 15.—Il dolce far niente.

NOVEMBER 16.—Idem.

NOVEMBER 17.—I rode down to Mr. Abbott's house, near Bairout, and bought cloth for a new suit of Arnäout clothing. I received a note from Maddox upon my return to Mansouree.

NOVEMBER 18, SUNDAY.—I walked up to Deir el Kalaa, to stay there with Maddox and St. John, and caught cold by sitting in a draught of cold air when I was heated by my walk. At night I felt feverish and unwell.

NOVEMBER 28.—To-day I arose, and ate for the first time since the 18th. I have been for the last ten days stretched upon the bed of sickness. A violent bilious fever, accompanied by ague, had nearly brought me to the tomb. My wretchedness was increased by a pitiless rain and storm, which poured in all around my devoted head, as I lay upon the damp ground, and by the total absence of every comfort, and almost every alleviation of misery. Had it not been for the kindness of Mr. St. John, who mixed my medicine for me and attended me, I know not what I should have done. The missionaries sent me some bark, and Mr. Abbott sent an emetic, and at length the friars (who had refused me on my first application,) lent me a mattress and a pair of tressels to raise me from the ground. What I have suffered during this painful period, I will not attempt to describe. I expected death, for my pulse was often at 130 and 140, and I was nearly delirious. I feared that brain fever would ensue, and I prayed heartily to God to avert this evil from me. I was fully prepared to die, but it has pleased him to spare me; and I am now rapidly recovering my strength and appetite. I am wasted to a mere shadow, by ten days' fasting and disciplining of the body. During the height of my fever, I one day took a little thermometer into my burning hand, the mercury was at 52, and rose in less than five minutes to 110! This will give you some idea of the heat of my blood.

NOVEMBER 29.—I am still mending rapidly, and walk about and eat with appetite, *malgré la pluie.*

NOVEMBER 30.—Snow upon Gebbail Sennin. The weather here is fine and sunny in the morning, but showery towards evening. My man Jiaccomo has fallen ill likewise, to increase my embarrassments. I see no chance of escaping from this country, and know not what will become of me. Meanwhile the letters from Constantinople are pacific, and there seems to be no prospect of war; so much the less chance have I of getting away, as now they will send nobody to take us off. I must, at all events, abandon for the present all thoughts of visiting the Holy Land; my late illness, the coming winter, the irritation of the public mind, the bad character of the Turks of that country, the approaching season of plague, &c. &c. are so many reasons against any movement in that direction. If I can get away to Alexandria, I may still see the Nile and its wonders, and even then, if so inclined, travel back to the Holy Land.

DECEMBER 1.—The weather is fine and cold, with a tramontane wind, which braces us up and invigorates our frames.

DECEMBER 2, SUNDAY.—A dreadful rain pours in all around us. The wind is excessively high. Notwithstanding these obstacles, I am recovering rapidly.

DECEMBER 3.—Northerly wind and finer weather. I sent St. John down to Mansouree to sound the Consul as to our going down to his country-house near Bairout, this dungeon being no longer tenable. He returned with a favourable answer. So we (St. John and myself) set off to-morrow morning, *Dio volente*, for that place.

DECEMBER 4.—I was awakened before daylight by a jackal, which came and put his nose under the door, and yelled and shrieked for a quarter of an hour. Ponto arose to pursue him, but could not get out. At about ten o'clock, St. John and I set off for Mr. Abbott's country-house, which we reached, after a tedious and dirty ride of three hours, in safety. All is tranquil in Bairout. The Austrian Consul sends me word of an opportunity for Alexandria, by a Tuscan brig from Saide and Sour. I shall avail myself of it, and propose setting off in a couple of days, accompanied by St. John, who wishes to go to Alexandria on his way to Malta. As soon as we can make our arrangements, we purpose hiring a camel to carry all our baggage, and setting off for Saide, where we hope to catch the brig. If not, we go on to Sour, where we shall be sure of her.

DECEMBER 5.—The weather is fine and mild. St. John went at my request to call on the Austrian Consul, and to consult with him. I wrote to the Sardinian Consul a letter of thanks, for getting my European baggage out of *sequester*,[*] and to Messrs. Maddox and Smith

---

[*] Poor Jacoub was nearly killed by an Arnäout soldier, while endeavouring to carry off my trunks. The ferocious Moslem beat him cruelly, and cut twice at him with his yatagan, dividing the shawl which he wore round his waist in two places, but fortunately not penetrating through all its folds.

about my horse. I was employed all the rest of the day in copying Arab, Druse, and Damascus costumes, from some very indifferent drawings made by a self-taught Greek artist. Poor St. John returned with an attack of fever upon him. I hope he will be well enough to move the day after to-morrow. I am not by any means well myself, and have been obliged to take more medicine.

We learn from M. Laurella, Austrian Consul, that the combined squadrons are waiting off the Dardanelles, in order, in the event of the Sultan's refusing to treat, to force that celebrated passage, and to dictate their terms under the walls of the Seraglio. Meanwhile, the Sultan says, he does not at all mind the loss of his fleet at Navarino, for that he can *build another;* and accordingly has *ordered a new one* to be made, as he would a new suit of clothes.

Owen Glendower.—" I can call spirits from the vasty deep.
Hotspur.—Ay! Uncle, but will they come?"

At night, rain, thunder, and jackals prevented my sleeping; add to these, the usual annoyance of fleas, which, wherever I go, are sure to prey upon me.

December 6.—I was employed during the whole rainy and tempestuous morning in colouring my costumes. I do not succeed; for it is so long since I have attempted any thing but pencilling, that I have almost forgotten the little which I did know of painting. I have failed in two attempts to sell my horse; and shall have to give him away to my servant when I embark; I am unlucky about horses. My tailor has not yet finished a suit of Arnäout clothing, which he has had in hand *eighteen days.* We learn that Ibrahim Pasha has marched with ten thousand men for Constantinople. If he have indeed evacuated the Morea, this will be a great step towards Grecian independence; but I can hardly credit the news.

December 7.—The weather is delightfully cool and clear. I was employed all the forenoon in drawing. In the evening a north-easterly wind.

December 8.—In the forenoon I went into Bairout, and called upon Laurella with St.

John. A strange brig is off the port; I hope she is destined to load here for Alexandria, and thus enable me, by getting on board of her, to avoid a tedious journey to Sour, to overtake the Tuscan vessel in which I had thought of going. I received a letter from Lady Hester Stanhope; most kind and solicitous about me, and was occupied all the evening in writing to her and to Chasseaud.

DECEMBER 9, SUNDAY.—The provoking vessel has passed on without coming into the port; and we shall still have to go by land to Saide and Sour. This morning a boat arrived from Cyprus, full of letters for the various Consuls; but, as far as I have heard, all remains in *statu quo*. I had the ever-disagreeable job of paying tailors and lacemen, who, after asking the exorbitant sum of five hundred and sixty-six piastres for their lace and labour, were too happy to accept four hundred and five; and, after all, I am told by competent judges, that I have paid a great deal too much. I have only found one honest man in the country, and that is my own servant.

Whatsoever enjoyment you may derive from visiting the East, it is poisoned by the continual attempts, on the part of the native population, to extort money from you, in all dealings which it may be your misfortune to have with them. Mule-drivers, ass-drivers, camel-drivers, tailors, shoemakers, bakers, porters, and, in short, every man with whom the common necessities of life bring you in contact; add to them the Sheiks, the Pashas and their rapacious dependents and attendants, all of whom expect presents from the unfortunate individual whose curiosity or whose fate may have thrown him into their hands, and you will form some idea of the constant drain that there is upon the traveller's purse, and the still more annoying trials to which his patience is put by the continual attempts, on all sides, to rob and deceive him. Add to all this the extreme pertinacity of the lower classes, in higgling for a para, about which they will make as much noise and vociferation as if the fate of the Ottoman empire depended upon its being paid to them. They cannot make the most ordinary contract with a traveller without changing their price (always augmenting upon the first one named) a dozen times, arguing and re-arguing, bawling and gesticulating for an hour: now after the traveller has made, as he thinks, the best possible bargain, he is sure, at the completion of the job, to be asked and tormented for more money, and this in a tone and manner which is quite insupportable. Baackshish! Baackshish! (buona màno! buona mano!) resounds from one end of the empire to the other.

December 10.—Fine weather; a man-of-war, supposed to be a corvette, is in sight to the south-west of Bairout point; I shall await her arrival ere I set out for Saide. To-day I received a visit from the Consul and the American missionaries. A messenger on a dromedary arrived in eleven days from Cairo, with a letter from Strangways to Mr. Abbott: all was well and quiet.

December 11.—The corvette is out of sight, owing to the thick weather. I still hope she is coming here.

December 12.—At daylight I had the

extreme satisfaction of descrying the corvette, under British colours, towing into the lower anchorage of Bairout; about noon I went on board of her with St. John; found her to be, as I had anticipated, the Pelorus from Alexandria. She is come here on purpose to see if any British or European subject should wish to leave the country, and to convey them, in that case, to Malta or Alexandria. She is to touch at Cyprus. Captain Richards, who commands her, is an old friend and shipmate of my brother Edward's, and has most kindly consented to take me away as well as St. John. Mr. Abbott came down in the evening, but did not go on board.

December 13.—Captain Richards came ashore after breakfast, and in the afternoon took me off to the ship; I found my old shipmate, Popham, second Lieutenant of the corvette. I had previously sent my baggage on board, under the care of my quondam squire, Jiaccomo, and had sold my horse for three hundred and ninety piastres to Maddox. I wrote yesterday afternoon another despatch to Lady

H. Stanhope, to inform her of the arrival of the Pelorus, and expressing her Captain's anxiety to be useful to her. The weather is threatening, and the swell is very heavy into the bay.

December 14.—At daylight we sailed for Cyprus. In the afternoon the wind light and baffling.

December 15.—Light breeze from northeast; at sunset we saw the high land of Cyprus.

December 16, Sunday.—In the afternoon, about five, we anchored in Larneca roads; heavy swell.

REMARKS ON SYRIA.

The sheep of Syria are of a remarkably large breed; their tails resemble those of the Cape sheep, and I have known them to weigh thirty pounds. It is ludicrous to see the manner of feeding these animals; this is all done by hand; their food, which consists of mulberry-leaves, is rolled up in the palm of the hand and stuffed into the animal's mouth, which suffers itself to be crammed very quietly, looking extremely complacent all the while. Its huge tail seems to be a great incumbrance to it, and is productive of certain disagreeable complaints, which require frequent ablutions, and which are performed by women or children. In short, the sheep is a much valued and highly petted animal, and seems to be quite conscious of its consequence and importance, stamping and butting at all dogs that may approach the door of its owner, near which it is generally tied up. The mutton is indeed excellent, and is preserved by the Arabs by boiling and potting it in large earthen jars, covered up with its own tallow or dripping, which is poured in a boiling state upon the meat as it lies in the jar.

Horned cattle in Syria are rare, and generally used for the plough; their flesh is rarely eaten by the Turks or Arabs, who generally prefer mutton.

The horse of the country is generally about fifteen hands high, strong and active, mostly of Syrian dams by Arab sires; the price varies from four hundred to two thousand piastres;

they are hardy, well-tempered, and sure-footed, have seldom any disorder, and live to a great age. They become extremely attached to the sieys, (or groom,) and will follow him as a dog will his master. Asses and mules are generally of a very superior description; and camels are numerous, but those of the coast not so large as those of the Desert.

The soil of Syria is very various. In the plains, near the coast, it is sandy; in the mountains, very rich, abounding with oxyde of iron, ironstone, limestone, and in many parts coal and volcanic substances. I have likewise, in many places in Mount Lebanon, found petrified sea-shells and marine substances.

The plain of the Backaā Metooalis might be the most fruitful in the world. Its loam of fine black earth indicates great vigour and richness. The country about Damascus abounds with fine pastures and corn land, and is well stocked with large trees, and watered by clear and rapid rivers. The climate of Syria is oppressively hot during the summer and autumn, and cold and rainy during the winter and spring.

Intermittent fever, accompanied by ague, the plague, and the dysentery, are frequent.

The seat of the Pashalick of Syria of the coast is Acre (the ancient Ptolemaïs.) This province has lately been enlarged by the addition of the little Pashalick of Tripoli in the east. Its inhabitants consist of Turks, Metooalis, Arabs of the Christian communion, Greeks, Jews, Druses, Ansyrians, or Ansari, and many other tribes. The Turks are numerically inferior to the Arabs; but they hold the sea-ports and fortresses, and govern more by fomenting the disunion of the various tribes than by force.

The Arabs of Mount Lebanon are under the temporal jurisdiction of the Emir Beshir, (Prince of the Druses,) who has lately become a convert to the Christian faith; more, it is said, from policy than conviction. They may be about two hundred thousand in number, and can easily bring twenty thousand armed men into the field. There have been of late years many bloody wars between the Emir Beshir and his cousin, the Sheik Beshir, chief of the Druse party, which ended in the total destruction and cruel death of the Sheik, and the almost entire extermination of his relatives, with the exception of his two little sons, who are in captivity at Acre, under the eye of the Pasha.

The widow of the Sheik Beshir once offered ten thousand purses to Abdallah Pasha for the liberation of her little sons. The crafty Turk encouraged the proposal, and gave the poor mother hopes; meanwhile he sent word to the Emir Beshir of the offer which had been made him, and bid him consider whether it were worth his (the Emir's) while to offer a larger sum for the safe detention of his captives. During this time the Sheik's wife had been induced, by the cunning Pasha, to pay the ten thousand purses in advance, and the Emir Beshir, dreading the consequences of delay, levied fifteen thousand purses upon his faithful subjects, which he immediately paid into the Pasha's treasury. The Turk kept the money of both parties, but did not release his captives.

The Arabs of Mount Lebanon have a very peculiar method of shooting the partridges, with which this district abounds. They make a slight square frame of wood, of about five feet in height, over which they stretch an ox-hide, perforated in three or four places. The ox-hide is moved quietly, in an upright position, along the ground; and the Arab, skulking behind it, is hidden from the view of the game, which unsuspectingly allow the sportsman to come within shot of them. The Arab, seeing through one of the apertures, protrudes quietly the muzzle of his long musket through another, beyond his shield, and firing upon the birds, as they feed in coveys upon the ground, kills a great many of them.

The Arabs are very economical of their powder and shot, both of which are of a very inferior description, and are manufactured in the mountains, particularly at Bsherri, near the celebrated Cedars.

They carry the powder in a sort of leather pouch having a neck and spring, in some degree resembling that of our European powder-horns, but without a measured charge, which they calculate by the eye, pouring it into the palm of the hand. Of shot, they put a very few grains into their gun, but it is very large.

They seem to be very expert marksmen. My servant, Jacoub, was a very keen sportsman, and indeed a good soldier; he had served in the wars between the Emir Beshir, and the Sheik Beshir of the Druses. "Aveva mangiato quatro palle di fusilia;" by which he meant that he had been four times wounded with musket-shot in these encounters.

He was a faithful, affectionate, and (for an Arab) honest fellow, and, I verily believe, would have fought for me, had there been occasion.

When we were among the Metooali of Naitra, and afterwards in the Bakaa, he seemed apprehensive of being attacked, and frequently examined the state of his arms, and cautioned me to be upon my guard.

In reply to his constant exhortation of "*Non ebbi paura Padrone,*" I used to remark, "I have no fear, Jacoub, for I have in my girdle two men's lives, in my double-barrelled gun two more, and in my sabre at least a dozen." This braggadoceio style I knew to be consonant to that of the people; and I was anxious, by assuming an appearance of fearlessness myself, to inspire my attendants with a similar feeling.

It is very material in the East, to the safety of the traveller, to go well armed, and for this obvious reason, that the predatory tribes are averse to spilling blood; the appearance therefore of arms, arguing in the wearer the ability and inclination to use them, shields him in general from the danger of attack. Let him beware, however, how he become the aggressor, and let him never be the first to spill blood, or to strike a blow. "The avenger of blood is behind him;" and a blow is never forgiven.

There are many serpents in Mount Lebanon. One day Ponto killed a very large one, which he found basking in the sun, at the foot of a bush. The dog had the sagacity to seize the animal by the back of the neck, close up to the head, and shook it until he had broken its spine. It was about four feet long, black on the back, and pale yellow on the belly. Its large flat head, lack-lustre grey eye, thick body, and inactive appearance, made me conjecture that it was not of a venomous nature. It looked more like a great lazy, slimy eel than a snake.

There are many gazelles in the mountain, but they are extremely shy. Quails, jays, the common rook, owls, some of which are extremely beautiful, woodpeckers, becca ficas, pigeons, hoopoes, linnets, goldfinches, and many European birds, abound.

I observed, during the heat of the day, in my journies in Syria, that Ponto suffered most extremely from it. He had however always the sagacity to run on a little before me, and place himself beneath the shade of some bush or stone, and here, as he lay panting for breath, and apparently quite exhausted, he would cover himself all over with the mould or sand, and thus enjoy a kind of earth bath.

The poor brute suffered also severely from

thirst; but as we always carried large earthen jars (of a porous nature, made at Bairout,) full of water for ourselves, we could generally spare him some to moisten his mouth and throat. In the mornings and evenings, which were always delightfully cool, he used to enjoy himself amazingly in hunting a stray jackal, gazelle, or flock of small birds.

He suffered also extremely from leeches (the ovæ of which, I suppose, he lapped up at the stagnant pools), and from ticks which adhered to his skin in great numbers. Indeed, I remember to have found one of these last half buried in my own right arm, near the shoulder.

It is surprising what pleasure a person, circumstanced as I was, without a companion, derived from the society of this dog, who always shared my humble meal, and slept at my feet upon the same carpet, covered up with the same cloak.

His vigilance at night, notwithstanding his fatigues by day, was extraordinary: he never suffered a mule or horse to move at his picket, without getting up to see what was the matter. The Bedouins, with whom I fell in from time to time, took a great fancy to him, and often offered to buy him. When Jacoub related anecdotes of the dog, the ignorant Bedouins, staring with amazement, vowed he was a magician.

At Baalbeck the Turks seemed to be much scandalized by my familiarity with him, and inquired the reason of my affection for an unclean animal. I replied to them in the words of Dr. Johnson, that the dog had been for four thousand years the intimate companion of man, but had learnt none of his vices; and, I added, that this animal, at all events, possessed a virtue unknown almost to man, namely, *fidelity*. They seemed struck by my answer, and said " *God is great.*"

It is easy to conceive how much I became attached to this animal: to him I could speak in English, and he alone appeared to understand me; of *his* fidelity I felt assured, and I knew that he would sacrifice his life to save mine. His care of my little convoy was quite remarkable; for if by chance Jacoub or the muleteer should lag behind, or if a mule or horse strayed for a moment out of the path, Ponto would turn back to find him; and when he had brought him up to the main body, then he would come forward to me, and, by his gambols and barking, show the pride he felt in having successfully performed what he conceived to be his duty.

The charm of the vagrant kind of life which I led for some weeks in Syria, is inconceivable; its constant variety, its perfect independence, the excitement of difficulty, the apprehension of danger, were so many powerful but agreeable stimulants. My wants were but few, and easily supplied; my bed was the ground, my covering a cloak, and my canopy the heavens; in such a climate I could desire no better. Yet I sometimes felt that solitude was very painful. It is so agreeable, says a witty Frenchman, to be able to say to one's companion, " *Voila un beau château!*" Pleasure is heightened by participation, and at times I own I did regret that I had no friend of similar habits and ideas, to partake of my delight in beholding lovely scenery, and to share my anxiety in the time of doubt and difficulty.

Nevertheless I gained one advantage from my solitude, namely, that of perfect liberty and independence; I halted when and where I chose, and set out again as my fancy dictated. I could live upon a morsel of Arab bread, and could content myself with a draught of water; and I could sit upon the back of my horse from an hour before day until nightfall, without feeling fatigued. I loved to wander amid the beauties of nature, and was fond of investigating the habits and character of man in all his varieties.

Of civilization I had seen enough. In the capitals of Europe, the manners of the world only differ by slight, and almost imperceptible degrees. He that has seen London, Paris, and Vienna, Rome, Naples, and Petersburgh, will find, that in all these cities, man is nearly the same creature of art, and living under the same common rule of the European compact.

In the East, all is widely different from the West; and here the European traveller finds a new mine to explore. How much I regret that circumstances obliged me to abandon this, to me, new and interesting field, I need not attempt to say. Should fortune reconduct me to the banks of the Bosphorus, I hope to pursue my peregrinations under more favourable auspices, for I now know what to do, and where to go. I now understand a little of the habits and prejudices of the East: I shall go better prepared and provided, and shall hope to profit more by my next journey than I have done by the last.

Of one thing I am firmly convinced, that the less baggage the traveller has, and the smaller his cortége, the better, for he then is unembarrassed in his movements, and does not become an object of cupidity to the ill-disposed, or to the predatory tribes. He should likewise, as much as possible, show a perfect confidence in the people among whom his fortune has thrown him, and carefully avoid giving them any offence by word or deed. Let him always be firm in resisting attempts upon his purse, or upon his property of every sort; and, above all things, let him never be prevailed upon to pay beforehand for any article whatever.

He will do well to learn a few Arabic or Turkish phrases of civility and salutation; always remembering that civility costs nothing, and that the Orientals are scrupulous observers of this sort of etiquette, and are favourably impressed by any stranger, who is gracious in his manners and kind in his speech.

He should also take great care not to speak in public to the females, nor to appear curious about them, nor intrusive in his observations upon them; the Orientals never forgive offences of this nature; nor are the women at all flattered by those marks of attention in public, which they might esteem very highly in private; for such demonstrations imply but little opinion of their chastity—a virtue most highly prized in the East.

The Englishman will find the Turks generally well disposed towards his nation; for, in despite of the present ambiguous nature of our proceedings towards them, they cannot forget past services rendered in the time of their necessity. He had better always make his attendants announce him as " el Inglis," in preference to " el Frangi," which is the general appellation of the European nations, with none of whom, excepting the *Muscovites*, are they so well acquainted as with ourselves.

Our countrymen have contrived likewise to establish a sort of prescriptive right *to do as they please* in Turkey, *as indeed every where else*, and Pasha Abdallah of Acre's reply to an observation of his Kehaya's, relative to a certain English traveller, who had the presumption to wear yellow boots and a white turban, " Dost thou not know that ' el Inglis ' has a right to do as he pleases in the dominions of the Sultan, as well as in Frangistan? if he wear his yellow boots upon his head, and his white turban upon his heels, what is that to thee !"

is strongly indicative of the disposition of the Turk to yield as much of his prejudices in our favour as he can.

. The principal expense to the Oriental traveller lies in his outfit of clothing, which ought to be handsome, if he intends to frequent the Seraïs of the Pashas and great men; and in the purchase of his horses: these last, however, if well taken care of, and not overworked, will always fetch him something at his journey's end.

He will find a good deal of jockeyship and duplicity, not unworthy of Newmarket or Epsom, displayed by the Turks upon occasions of purchase or sale of horses; they frequently procure a number of their friends to come, as by accident, and puff off the horse in question, bidding against the traveller, and showing a great apparent anxiety to purchase themselves; in these cases, the only plan is to get backed likewise by another party, who decry the animal, and affect to find *unfavourable marks* about him. The Turks and Arabs are so superstitious in these matters, that they will not trust themselves upon a horse which has a *bad mark* about him; this being sure to portend some evil to the rider. The traveller may thus get a good horse cheap.

In general, the Arabs will not part with their *best horses*—these are too precious to be sold; they prize the mares more than the horses; but in the case of a *bad mark*, they will sell them for a mere trifle.

The Kings of France and Bavaria send experienced horse-dealers into Syria to purchase Arab stallions for the European haras. I never met with these agents; but I am told by good judges, who have seen them and their cattle, that they have in general been much taken in. Indeed, *good horses* upon the coast are very difficult to be had: the plains of the Houran afford the best market; but they are distant, and not much visited by European merchants.

When the Emir Beshir had succeeded in quelling the revolt of the Druses, headed by Sheik Beshir, and had put this chieftain (although his cousin) to death, he determined to wreak his vengeance upon the remaining adherents of the Sheik, among whom were two of his uncles. He put out the eyes of the one, and cut out the tongue of the other.

The executioner of these acts of barbarity clumsily performed the latter operation, and left so much tongue remaining in the victim's mouth, that he could still curse the Emir.—" The dog speaks!" said the Prince: "another inch." The mutilated organ was again pulled out with pincers and again shortened!

When I was at Teddin, I saw a man, apparently of rank, sitting down upon the ground, in front of the palace, fixing his sightless-looking eyes upon the evening sun, in the manner peculiar to blind people. It struck me that this personage might be the Druse chieftain whose eyes had been cruelly put out by the Emir.—I asked the question of my servant; but he, being a subject of the Emir's, did not dare to answer, but dexterously got rid of the subject.

The only palliation for such enormities as these, is to be found in this consideration, that had the vanquished been the victors, they would have done exactly the same thing.

I regret to say that I could collect very little information respecting the religious tenets and practices of the Druses.

Padre Modesto seemed inclined to think that they worshipped the true God, but were deists: he said that they were divided into three classes: the Akhals, or sacerdotal order, distinguished by their white turban; initiated; and the vulgar, or uninitiated; that like the Freemasons, these separate classes could distinguish each other by a secret sign, but that the lower grades did not know the secrets of the higher, and that each class had *sacred books* belonging to their grade, the uninitiated not understanding the books and mysteries of the initiated, and these, in their turns, not understanding those of the Akhals; that they occasionally met together in the open air to celebrate their religious ceremonies, which seemed to consist of a kind of exhortation from the Akhals, and in the distribution of figs and raisins, to the eating of which some mystical signification was attached.

The Druses never forgive a public insult or a blow; and they are said to be great observers of their word. They are a fierce and numerous tribe, and can bring ten thousand armed men into the field.

I have been favoured, by a friend of mine, (an Oriental traveller,) with a few notes upon this interesting topic, collected by himself in Syria, both from native Syrians and European residents in that country.

"The word Druse signifies initiated. The country occupied by the Druses is about one hundred and thirty leagues in extent; from Nahr el Kelb to Sour, and between the valley of Bhar el Hamer and the sea, it is divided into seven districts, of which Deir el Kamaār is the capital.

"Since the death of the Sheik Beshir, the Druses have had no particular chief. They are divided into Occals, learned initiates, and ignorant.

"The religion of the Druses is a mixture of Christian and Oriental doctrines—Metempsychosis seems to be the principal dogma.

"They hold that the infant in the womb is merely matter, and nourished by matter; that at its birth it receives the spirit of some departed one. The soul passes always from one of the same religion to another of the same; thus a Christian initiated cannot be happy in the next life, because his soul always returns into the body of a Christian; and therefore they care not to make proselytes. They believe that at the end of the world they will be placed above all people.

"If the soul of a Druse initiated passes into the body of an uninitiated, he is sure to be initiated in the course of his life.

"The soul passes successively into many bodies, until it is sufficiently purified; but the souls which are incorrigible pass into the bodies of animals.

"They are bound to speak the truth, to believe in one God—never to believe in any other religion, nor to reveal the mysteries of their own.

"When a Druse wishes to arrive at the highest pitch of initiation, it is necessary to make a confession of all the bad actions of his life, before an assembly of the Occàls.

"There are some Druses in the Houran, behind Aleppo. They pretend to have some sectaries of their religion in India, and even in Europe!"

Burckhardt and Jowett give pretty nearly the same information upon this head; and I fear that I have learnt nothing new about it. I made two or three unsuccessful attempts to worm some of the secrets out of Lady Hester Stanhope; but she detected me, and was always afterwards upon her guard with me upon this topic. I think she is likely to know a good deal about the religion of this singular people, from her intimate knowledge of them, and her acquaintance with the late Sheik Beshir.

The Ansyrians, or Ansari, seem to be immersed in all the disgusting sensualities of Paganism,

Their religious rites are said to consist of the relics of the worship of *Venere Astarte*, the Syrian Venus. There are many other sects among the inhabitants of the mountains, for a description of which, refer to Burckhardt and Jowett.

CHAPTER IV.

Departure for, and arrival at, Alexandria.—I am obliged to abandon my project of ascending the Nile.—Arrival of the *débris* of the Turco-Egyptian fleet from Navarino.—Visit to the Antiquities of Alexandria.—We sail with convoy for Malta.—Arrival at Malta.—Quarantine.—La Valetta.—Carnival gaieties.—Opera.—Presentation of the Flag of Saint George.—Preparations for departure for Sicily and Italy.

DECEMBER 17.—Fresh breezes from northeast; very heavy swell and tremendous surf all round the harbour. I am attacked with fever and ague. Calomel and salts and starvation.

DECEMBER 18.—Fresh gales. It was impossible to get the wine for ship's use off, on account of surf. I am better. In the afternoon we weighed for Alexandria. Fresh gales and heavy sea. Rain and squalls all night.

December 19.—Ditto weather. I am again attacked, and very unwell indeed. In the evening, in reefing topsails, two boys fell out of the mizen rigging overboard, and in spite of the most prompt succour with life-buoy and boats, one was unfortunately drowned. The night squally and rainy.

December 20.—Fine weather. I am convalescent, but extremely weak and languid.

December 21.—Fever and ague and illness all day.

December 22.—I am convalescent. We arrived at Alexandria. The weather was too cold and boisterous to allow of my looking much about me. I saw, however, Pompey's pillar. I have no letters from England; but one from Smyrna, with a small credit upon Messrs. Briggs and Co. I can gain no certain information about Strangways.

December 23.—I was attacked early in the

morning, about half-past one, with the ague and fever, which lasted until nearly eight o'clock. I am extremely reduced and wretched. Arrived His Majesty's ship Philomel, Captain Keith, from Malta with convoy. He was in the affair of Navarino. Still no letters for me. Weather stormy and uncertain.

DECEMBER 24.—I am convalescent, and the weather is mending. Keith dined on board, and I was allowed to drink four glasses of wine. I take sulphate of quinine three times a day, and am to-day better.

DECEMBER 25.—Thank God! I have this day broken the chain of the fever. Up to this moment, half-past ten, I have had no return of the malady. I have, however, upon due deliberation and consultation with Dr. Huey, of the ship, resolved upon abandoning all idea of prosecuting my travels in the East; for who shall say when and where this malady may not return upon me; and what can a man see or discover in this world which can recompense him for the loss of his health? We are going shortly with convoy to Malta, where I shall repose in quarantine twenty-five days; rather too long a period for a person burning to partake again of the pleasures and comforts of civilized life. I enjoyed a social dinner in the gun-room extremely.

December 26.—Thank God! I have no return of the fever. I now hope that the disorder is overcome. The weather is stormy and disagreeable. I cannot venture to go on shore, being sure of getting a ducking, which might bring on a return of my malady. Thus I shall leave Egypt without having put my foot upon its sands. I cannot control fate. We learn again from Syra, that the allied Ambassadors have left Constantinople, and are on board the squadron below the castles at Smyrna. Encore une raison de plus pour ne pas continuer mes voyages.

December 27.—The weather is fine and more moderate. I am, thank God! rapidly recovering my health and strength. We go to sea to-day. In the afternoon the wind blowing right in, and the appearance of the Egyptian fleet off the port, prevented the pilots from taking us out.

DECEMBER 28.—Cold and blowy. I feel aguish and unwell. This day came in the remains of the Turco-Egyptian fleet from Navarino, consisting of four very large corvettes, two frigates,* and some brigs and transports. Most of the men-of-war are jury-rigged and a good deal cut up, but some have not been at all engaged. There are still two frigates outside, which cannot beat up to the passage, being jury-masted. We observed a good many Greek women and children on board the transports. I dined on board the Philomel, and became acquainted with her first Lieutenant, Lord E. Russel.

DECEMBER 29.—It still blows a gale from

---

* One of the frigates had a boat with a blue flag in the bow, hoisted up astern. Captain Richards hearing of this, and suspecting that it was one of the Asia's boats, sent and claimed it of the Pasha, who ordered it to be given up, which was acccordingly done; the boat was hoisted into the Pelorus, and carried to Malta.

the westward, and we hold on. I am better. The two frigates cannot get in, and must bear up for Aboukir.

DECEMBER 30, SUNDAY.—Strong breezes from the westward. I don't think we shall have a change of wind and weather until the full moon, and expect to see the new year open upon us at Alexandria. I have not yet been able to go on shore, the weather being too boisterous to admit of landing, without getting wet to the skin, which would not at all agree with the present state of my health.

DECEMBER 31.—Weather more moderate, (thermometer 47°). I went on shore with Captains Richards and Keith to see Pompey's Pillar and Cleopatra's Needles. We landed at the Mahmoudia, and walked through groups of miserable and dirty Arabs, until we procured three donkies; upon these we rode over the sand-hills and, *opus incertum,* to the immense and beautiful Corinthian column ycleped (nobody knows why) Pompey's Pillar. It is indeed a wonderful specimen of what the ancients could do:

first, as to its immensity, the shaft being about ninety feet high, of one solid piece of red granite; and secondly, as respects their knowledge of the mechanical powers, for I much doubt, whether, with all our science, in these degenerate days, we could raise and place such an enormous mass upon its pedestal. The capital appeared to me to be of a bad Corinthian, the acanthus leaf being very rudely and plainly carved.

This noble monument of the arts is much disfigured by the bad taste of my countrymen and brother sailors, who have bedaubed its elegant shaft all over with their names and those of their ships, in black characters; it is to be feared likewise that it will some day be thrown down by the indiscreet and barbarous thirst for coins, which has induced many a *civilized Goth* to do that which is alone worthy of Turks and Arabs, in undermining the base of the shaft and pedestal. I was disappointed in the two obelisks of red granite, called Cleopatra's Needles; they stand (or rather one stands, and the other lies) in too low a situation to make any figure, and the eye does not do justice to their height and proportions; probably, too, the contrast between the polished orders of the Greek and the barbarous conceptions of the Egyptian, was unfavourable to these celebrated obelisks. We rode round the walls to the Eastern Port, and had a good view of the ancient and modern Pharos. Vast quantities of brick-work, and pieces of precious marbles, &c. denote that this was once a splendid emporium, and not, as at present, the seat of squalour, dirt, and misery. We saw some excavations for hydraulic purposes, in which were vast masses of the solid masonry of the Romans; and I discovered part of an Egyptian statue of the black basaltic-looking stone, in which most of their statuary is executed. We did not enter the town, having no particular desire to expose ourselves to insults, which, now the remainder of their fleet is returned from Navarino, were likely enough to be heaped upon us. In returning on board, we got a good wetting, the gale having returned with renewed vigour. I dined on board the Philomel, and met M. d'Oysenville, of His Christian Majesty's ship Vestale.

January 1, 1828.—Strong gales; struck top-gallant masts, and pointed the yards to the wind. In the evening, heavy rain and squalls. (Thermometer 45.)

January 2.— Ditto weather, with heavy rain.

January 3.—More moderate; we attempted to get the convoy under weigh, but failed.

January 4.— We sailed for Malta, with about seven sail of convoy.

We had bad weather almost all the way, and foul winds nearly the whole time. Nothing particular occurred during our passage. We got a fair wind on the 19th, on the south coast of Candia; it soon increased to a gale.

We reached Malta on the morning of the 21st of January, and went into the quarantine harbour of Marsamucetto; here we are to remain until the 9th of February. I went on the following day to look at the lazaretto, intending to take up my quarters there, not thinking it fair to trespass any longer upon Captain Richards's hospitality; but on the following day I was again attacked by the fever and ague, which obliged me to abandon all ideas of quitting the ship, the lazaretto quarters presenting nothing but stone floors, arched roofs, and no fireplaces.

JANUARY 24.—I am again attacked, and now must make up my mind for some days' suffering.

JANUARY 25.—I am convalescent; but tomorrow expect the fever again. I fear that this disagreeable companion will prevent my travelling in Sicily, as I had intended. I went this day with Captain Richards to the Parlatorio, and saw there my old shipmate Dilke, who was at Navarino, and on that brilliant day earned his promotion.

JANUARY 26.—Ague and fever all day.

JANUARY 27.—Convalescent. Wrote long letters to England, to send by the returning packet.

FEBRUARY 5 and 6.—Gales from the N. E.

with rain. On the 5th arrived His Majesty's ship Alacrity, with convoy from Smyrna; she is our companion in captivity.

February 8.—This evening the Captain of the quarantine department came to inform us that our captivity had expired, and that we were at liberty to depart for the inner harbour to-morrow morning.

Let me here return my sincere thanks to the Captain and Officers of the Pelorus, for their unremitting kindness and hospitality to me, who have been so long a guest on board of their happy little ship. Circumstanced as I am, ill of a fever, and thrown by chance upon their hands, I cannot appreciate too highly the service they have rendered to me.

February 9.—At four in the morning we slipped from the buoy in the quarantine harbour, and towed and swept the ship round into the great harbour of Valetta. Here we arrived about half-past five.

All is movement and gaiety in this beautiful port, in which are at present four Russian sail of the line, and several English men-of-war. After breakfast we towed the ship up into the dock-yard creek, nearly rubbing our side against the houses on the right hand as we went.

At eleven o'clock Popham and myself went on shore to Valetta, accompanied by my faithful companion old Ponto, who was almost mad with delight, in getting on shore once again. We clambered over the immense flights of stone stairs, (vulgarly called *Nix mangiare,*) and went through handsome streets to Beverley's hotel, where I found good (but too roomy and cold) apartments.

I called upon the Admiral, and was presented to Lady Codrington. I paid my visit of ceremony to the Lieutenant-Governor, and walked about the beautiful city and ramparts with Popham. We went to see Governor Ball's monument and tomb.

The monument is a pretty little square Doric temple, surrounded by fluted columns, supporting their appropriate entablature, having an inscription in Latin. In each front of the building is a niche, with a statue of some allegorical Divinity. It is, on the whole, a pretty structure, but stands upon too high a basement, which makes its proportions appear faulty. It is situated upon the *Saluting battery.* The tomb is further round towards the quarantine harbour, and presents nothing remarkable, but a very long Latin inscription.

I returned home about four, very tired, and my feet aching from wearing European boots, (for I was now Christianized.) Popham dined with me; and at eight o'clock we went to the opera, " *Il Barbiere di Seviglia.*" The performance was tolerable, the house small, but neat, and well lighted, it being a benefit night, *con piena illuminazione.* We had a solo on the violoncello, by il Signor Salvatore Amore, not above mediocrity. I discovered my Munich friend, Count Scebberas, *un des anciens Preux*, in one of the boxes; he left Munich in October, and has been here ever since.

FEBRUARY 10.—I was confined all the day

to my room, by a return of my fever and ague, but in the evening I was so much better, as to be able to dine at the Admiral's.

FEBRUARY 11.—In the evening the Captain and officers of the Pelorus, and Captain Dilke, dined with me. Afterwards we went to Lady E. Ponsonby's ball at the Palace. Here are some very handsome rooms and tapestry. The Maltese women are generally plain. I remained at the ball until midnight.

FEBRUARY 12.—This morning I was again attacked by fever and ague while in bed. The Rattlesnake has arrived from Carabousa; she brings the account of the capture of that island, but of the total loss of the Cambrian, who got on shore in going into the harbour, from missing stays. The officers and crew are all saved.—Poor Captain Hamilton! this is a sorrowful winding up for you, after all the anxiety and trouble which you have had in the Levant! The Zebra is likewise arrived; her Captain has just died of a brain fever.

I rose from my bed about half-past one, very

weak and languid. I went in the evening with Popham to the opera, "*La Schiava di Bagdad.*" One of the duets between the sopran and the tenor was delightful; but I have heard it before in the Azillia, "*Al punto estremo, al punto estremo Io t'amero.*" I know not whether Rossini or Paccini has the merit of this delightful composition.

FEBRUARY 13.—This morning I am convalescent, and hope to be able to get out and take a little exercise. I went to the Parlatorio to see Captains Hamilton and Bridgeman, who are at present in quarantine. I saw some of the officers of the Cambrian, but found the damp and vaulted rooms of the Parlatorio too cold to allow of my staying long there, and I was disappointed in not seeing the two Captains, who did not come on shore.

FEBRUARY 14.—The weather rainy and squally. At eleven o'clock the minute guns announced the funeral procession of poor Captain Cotton. The gloomy state of the weather is quite in accordance with the melancholy occasion.

FEBRUARY 15.—We are all occupied in selecting characters and dresses for a masked ball, to be given on the 18th, at the Palace (for 'tis the height of the Carnival). I am to personate, first, a young boarding-school Miss (for which character I must sacrifice my Turkish moustache); second, a Troubadour; and third, Ibrahim Pasha: for the two latter personages I must have recourse to *une moustache postiche*.

FEBRUARY 18.—I was dress-hunting all the morning; but failed in procuring a proper costume for the Troubadour. I dined at Major Hewett's, an old friend of mine who belongs to the Rifles, and met there Colonel Brown and Captain Symonds. After dinner we had great fun in dressing ourselves for the masked ball at the Palace. We, and almost all the Rifles, are to represent a girls' school out walking; the mistress was Colonel Brown, the teachers, Major Hewett and Captain Symonds. The whole school rendezvoused at Colonel Bathurst's; and never was there so extraordinary a looking set of young ladies brought together.

The ball was very splendid, and well attended; and there were some excellent masks. In the course of the evening, Popham, Portman, and myself, dressed *à la Turque*, and, we are told, we made a very good group. I returned home at five in the morning.

FEBRUARY 19.—This day was holden a grand tournament in honour of the Lady Anne di Comino.* The knights were ten in number, and were armed in complete steel, from the armoury of the order of Malta, in the Palace. The Lady Anne was personated by Mr. Grey, (Mid of the Talbot,) attended by a Mameluke (myself); the Grand Marshal was Colonel Bathurst, extremely well dressed in the style of Charles the First. The procession from the Palace to the grand square was as follows:

* Comino is a small island belonging to the Government of Malta, and is celebrated for immense numbers of rabbits, which are the sole inhabitants of the isle.

LA VALETTA. 207

Two Lancers to clear the way.
Two Trumpeters.
A Mameluke.
The Lady Anne di Comino.
The Grand Marshal.
An Officer of the Lists.
Knights, two and two.

We rode round through the principal streets to show ourselves to the people, and drew up in the grand Square, opposite the Palace, as below.

Officer of the List.
G. Marshal,   Lady Anne,   Mameluke.

Knights at their barrier.   Knights at their barrier.

CAREER.

Two Trumpeters.

Palace.

Several courses were run, and many spears broken; after which a very spirited encounter with swords took place. The prize (a fat rabbit) was awarded gracefully by the fair Lady Anne to Colonel Brown (Georgio di Bruneleschi dei Verdi), amid the cheers of the assembled population of Valetta. We now formed in grand procession, marched once round the Square, and through the great gates of the Palace into the principal court-yard, where we dismounted, and accompanying the fair Lady Anne di Comino, proceeded to the state-rooms, where we partook of a splendid collation. No accident happened in the lists, and the whole went off remarkably well. It was a very pretty sight, and seemed to afford great entertainment to the Maltese. Thus ended the Carnival.

FEBRUARY 20.—I rode out to St. Antonio, with Captain Ferguson, of the Rifles. This is a *maison de plaisance* of the Governor's, with a beautiful garden.

I remained at Malta until the beginning of

May, slowly recovering my health and strength, and awaiting letters from England, and the arrival of my friend, Captain Dalling, from the Levant, who had not long since been promoted, and was likely to return home overland. In him I hoped to find a *compagnon de voyage*.

The officers of the rifle brigade, one battalion of which is stationed here, were so good as to make me an honorary member of their mess, as indeed they do all Captains of men-of-war on the Mediterranean station. This was a great blessing to me, who required generous living and convivial society.

From the Lieutenant-Governor, the Admiral, Sir E. Codrington, and the Commissioner, I received the greatest possible kindness; and the hospitalities of the many amiable families in Valetta were showered upon me in profusion; in short, I was in perfect clover; and had my health been good, I should have enjoyed my stay at Malta excessively.

I had the advantage of becoming acquainted with Admiral Count Heyden, on board of whose flag-ship, the Azoff, a very imposing and beautiful ceremony took place, on the 6th of April, namely, the presentation of the flag of St. George; an honour which had not been conferred on any occasion since the days of Peter the Great, excepting upon the battalions of the Imperial Guard, during the first occupation of Paris by the allied armies.

About ten o'clock in the morning, the beautiful harbour of Valetta was covered with the barges of state belonging to the Lieutenant-Governor, the authorities of the island, the British Admiral and his Captains, and those of the commanders of the Russian men-of-war, all of whom were seen repairing, in great pomp, on board the Azoff, to compliment Count Heyden on the occasion.

The Admiral and the General were received with the customary salutes and honours, the yards of the Azoff being manned, and all her officers and ship's company dressed in handsome uniforms and military caps.

The visits of ceremony over, high mass, according to the rites of the Greek Church, was celebrated upon the quarter-deck; the banner of St. George was brought out in great state, and blessed by the officiating priest, and the officers and crew sworn to defend it to their last gasp; for this flag cannot be surrendered to an enemy.

The walls, ramparts, tops of houses, and spires of churches in Valetta, were crowded with the population in holiday costume: the day was perfectly serene, the sky without a cloud, the sea as blue as azure, and not a breath stirred in the heavens.

Suddenly the yards and mast-heads of all the Russian squadron are covered with men; the banner of St. George waves its silken folds over the poop of the Azoff; five hundred pieces of cannon rend the air with their thunder in majestic salutes. The hulls of the ships, and soon the yards, disappear in clouds of white smoke; the men on the royal mast-heads alone, are seen suspended, as it were, in the mid-heaven; the echoes of Valetta and the Cottonera repeat the sound of the cannon ten thousand times. Then follows a deep silence, until the batteries of Sant Elmo, and all the lines of Malta, with the guns of the British ships-of-war in their turn, pay the tribute of their homage to the flag of the patron Saint of Christendom. The whole population is at the highest pitch of enthusiasm; the waving of handkerchiefs, and the voices of thousands, lend their aid to celebrate the festival.

Again the guns of the Azoff open their fire, in acknowledgment of the honour conferred upon her nation by her British friends; and then the sounds of martial music, from the various military bands, succeed to the roar of the cannon. I shall never forget this scene.

APRIL 12.—Count Heyden gave a magnificent *dejeuné à la fourchette* on board of the Azoff, at which the Lieutenant-Governor, Lady Emily Ponsonby, Sir Edward and Lady Codrington, all the authorities, naval, military, and civil, and the elite of Valetta, attended. The quarter-deck was fitted up for a ball, in great style; and the dancing and feasting continued until ten o'clock at night.

During the evening, his Majesty's ship Talbot, Hon. F. Spencer, sailed for Marseilles, and some of us went a long way out to sea in Colonel Brown's (of the Rifles) pleasure-boat; we could not however catch her, and returned to the Azoff to dance mazourka and cotillions.

APRIL 31.—I went to a great pic-nic, at Crendi, the country-house of Colonel Gardner. Here are some curious remains of a Druidical or Celtic temple.

The rest of my stay at Malta was very well disposed of, at dinners, pic-nics, balls, &c. &c. My friend Dalling arrived, and purified in the lazaretto, and agreed, after a few days' stay at Valetta, to accompany me homewards by Sicily, Italy, and Germany.

On the 7th of MAY, I took leave of all my kind friends at Malta, and prepared for starting on the morrow by a steam-packet, which had arrived from Naples on the 4th, and returns thither by Messina. This was too fine an opportunity to lose, and I had received the *necessary letters* from my agent in England.

Malta is so well known as a fortress of the first order, and as one of the best ports in the world, that I have not presumed to give any account of it, being well aware that I have nothing new to say about it. But before I take my leave of Valetta, I must observe, that it is one of the most agreeable cities I was ever in. The Maltese* are an industrious, sober, orderly, and active people, and the English residents form the most hospitable and agreeable society which I have ever met with in the Colonies; indeed it would give me great pleasure to pay them another visit.

The metropolitan Church of St. John is a perfect bijou, encrusted with rich Mosaic, and ornamented with splendid tombs of the Knights of Malta. Here are likewise preserved the keys of the fortress of Rhodes.

* The Maltese speak a dialect of Arabic, and still wear the long red cap or tarboosh of their ancestors of the Desert. Their history is involved in the impenetrable mist of remote antiquity.

CHAPTER V.

Etna, Taormina and Messina.—Stromboli.—Capri and Vesuvius.—Arrival at Naples.—Visit to Pompeia.- Recent discoveries.—Studio.—Vases, bronzes, &c. &c.—Departure for Rome.—Appearance of the country.—Doganieri.—Arrival at Rome.—Recent improvements. —Antiquities, &c. &c.—Studios of Sculptors.—Departure from Rome. —Nepi and Civita Castellano.—Loss of Ponto.—Terni.—Foligno.—Nostra Signora D. A.—Perugia.—Lake of Thrasimene.—Ramaggio.—Florence.—Gallery.--Palazzo Cetti. —Cascine, &c. &c.—I recover Ponto.—His adventures.

On Thursday, the 8th of May, our party, consisting of Captains Dalling and Dilke, of the navy, and Mr. Hall, an Oriental traveller, left Malta, on board the steam-boat, Ferdinand of Naples, at mid-day, for Sicily. The weather was hot, with a strong sirocco, and a swell from the south-east. We fell in with and passed close to His Majesty's ship the Revenge. The swell made the vessel roll and tumble about a good deal, and very soon drove me down sick into my berth. How unlucky, that one, whose profession is the sea, should always suffer so much from the *maladie de mer!* In the evening, as we drew in towards Cape Passaro, the swell subsided, and I came on deck, and became acquainted with some of our fellow-passengers; among whom was Admiral Taylor, who remembers my paternal grandfather, Sir Thomas Frankland, at that time high up among the admirals; and Dr. Nott, who was an intimate friend of my father's, and his contemporary at Christ Church.

May 9.—At daylight, we were close under Mount Etna; the view was noble and imposing; and there was some smoke at the crater. We stood into the bay under Taormina, and had a very fine view of its celebrated theatre, and the old Gothic and Saracenic walls and towers which surround it.

Here we landed some of our passengers, and gazed for an hour or so upon the magnificent scenery before us, and the coast of Calabria, on our right hand. Among the passengers I found some German acquaintances, Count Chorinski, and Prince Tour and Taxis. At one o'clock we reached Messina, and after some difficulty with the boatmen, we landed at the Custom House, and being officers of the Real Marina Britannica, were passed through immediately, without any search, whilst the German Counts and Princes were examined rigorously.

Nothing can exceed the beauty of the port of Messina, with its Faro and fortresses; its convents, churches, and mountains. Indeed the church seems to thrive in this land of milk and honey. We went to the Gran Bretagna, and were well lodged and fed. After dinner we strolled along the Marina, and lionized the city, enjoying extremely the beauty of this celebrated strait and its adjacent mountains, and took our coffee and ices at a café on the Marina, where we saw our friend Dr. Nott. We retired to bed at an early hour.

May 10.—We were employed all the morning in arranging our plans and getting our passports from consuls, police-officers,* intendants, &c. &c. and in booking ourselves for Naples by the steamer. After dinner we took a delightful walk down to the Esplanade, on the south side of the city, from whence we had a most superb view of the city, with its old and modern fortifications, of the former, more particularly the tower built by Richard Cœur de Lion, when he occupied this city on his way to the Crusades. At night some of our party went to a *soireé dançante*. It is difficult to conceive any thing more beautiful than the view of the coast of Calabria on a clear evening, and of the tranquil blue strait which washes its shores. Reggio, and many other towns (well remembered by some of our British sailors and soldiers,) dotted along the side of the mountains, while

* We found all these authorities civil and obliging.

Scylla and the Faro seem almost to block up the entrance of the narrow passage which divides Sicily from Italy.

To-day we called upon Dr. Nott, but missed him, he calling upon us at the same time.

May 11.—This morning our companion, Mr. Hall, left us to make the tour of Sicily. I own that I did wish to accompany him, and had indeed determined upon visiting Etna, Taormina, Catania, Syracuse, Girgenti, Sigestum, Palermo, &c.&c., but the heat, the lateness of the season, the deal of work I have to get through in Italy and Germany, added to my late illness, and the determination of my friends Dalling and Dilke, to go straight to Naples, decided me to relinquish the project for the present; and reflecting that one cannot see all the world, I was obliged to put up with my disappointment. This morning we lionized the cathedral, which is remarkable for some ancient Mosaic, very perfect and good of its kind, and some singularly ugly antique columns, all of different orders, if orders such ugly composite could be called. The principal doorway is a handsome specimen of florid Gothic, and is in good preservation. In front of the cathedral, a little to the right, stands a handsome fountain, the upper basin of which is supported by four pretty female figures, which have been so contrived as to give out the water in a *very natural manner,* but at present it spouts out a little below them from four dolphins. (This fountain is in much better taste than that of the Mannechi pisse at Brussels.) We next went down to the Esplanade of yesterday, to sit under the shady trees and make a sketch; which done, we clambered up on some old and demolished works, and examined the position, and enjoyed the extreme beauty of the scenery and the weather. Our friend, Dr. Nott, is gone to-day in a speronara to Palermo, by Céfalu and Termini. In the evening we walked upon the Marina, and patronized the ices at the café. There is a fine frigate lying close to the beach to *protect the commerce of Sicily against pirates.*

May 12.—At 10, in the morning, we embarked on board the steamer for Naples, after fighting a great battle at the inn, where we were charged an exorbitant price, of which we docked off a third. Our passage through the Faro was one of the most beautiful things imaginable; and the view of the city, embayed as it is, and backed by its lofty and irregularly-shaped mountains, covered with wood, and vines, and verdure, was quite equal to any scenery I have ever beheld. As we passed along, we saw all the Martello towers and forts raised by the English army of Sicily; and our friend Dalling, who had served here in the Amphion, with Sir William Hoste, was able to point out to us many interesting spots. We hove-to for about a quarter of an hour off the outer Faro, and took on board a quantity of *sword-fish* for the market at Naples. These animals were very large, and are an object of great importance to the trade of Messina, selling very high indeed at Naples. They are taken by the harpoon, a man looking out at the mast-head of the boats, announcing their approach, and even striking them from thence. On quitting the Faro we saw the Lipari islands, and at about four o'clock passed close to Stromboli, which was smoking away, and throwing up occasionally a few large stones. This island seems to be very fertile, and produces a vast number of vines: it is extremely picturesque, but its volcano disappointed my expectation. As the night advanced, we saw it to a greater advantage. The weather was delightful, and the sea as smooth as glass; and, thank God, I was not sea-sick.

May 13.—At daylight off Capri. This island presents a very rugged and picturesque appearance towards the south, and one very remarkable detached rock, pierced through by an arch, which looks as if it had been hewn by the hand of man. At nine, we passed Capo di Minerva, looking green and beautiful, with its old gothic towers and breast-works. On rounding this headland, we opened upon Vesuvius, which was smoking, but tranquil, and not looking as terrific as it did when I last saw it in 1820, when there was a splendid irruption. The change in the conformation of its biforked summit was very conspicuous, the crater having fallen in, and being now nearly as low as Monte Somma. Torre del Greco, embosomed in vineyards and black masses of lava, looked smiling and prosperous, with its white houses and red roofs; and this ever beautiful scene was rendered dear to my imagination from the recollections of passed days and departed friends.

We reached the anchorage off the Bella Napoli at about 10. 30., and found ourselves surrounded by noble-looking men-of-war, which seem to be kept here, not for use, but for show. The officer of the Sanità, who came alongside, would not give us pratique on account of some goods which were brought from Malta, and which it seems were *ogetti sospetti;* the fact is, the government of Naples * does not like much intercourse between its dominions and those of Great Britain in the Mediterranean, and it wishes to throw every obstacle in its power to such intercourse, and, by petty vexations, to put a stop to it. After a delay of two hours, during which time people *came on board and went ashore with the swordfish,* we were allowed to disembark, after having our passports exchanged for a biglietto di la polizia. Our baggage was gently treated by the custom-house people, who, upon hearing that we were Uffiziali superiori della Marina Britannica, said that we should be used con tutta decenza. We drove to the Albergo della Vittoria, which enfilades the gardens of the Chiaja; and here we were tolerably lodged

* There is another and perhaps stronger, reason for the dislike manifested by the Government of Naples to the intercourse kept up by the steam-boat, namely, that the Court has several shares in a *sailing packet* company. It does not therefore like its steam competitor.

"au second." In the evening we lounged in the Villa Reale, and retired at an early hour to bed.

May 14.—Visits at the minister's and consul's engrossed the morning. I wrote a long letter to my mother and sisters. We went to see some carriages at Sig. Angrisani's, a kind of speculator in post-horses and vehicles for all Italy, but saw nothing which would suit us. In the evening we drove to the Mergellina, and walked in the gardens of the Chiaja, where I was introduced to Sir G. and Lady Airey, friends of my family's. At night we went to the Fondo, to see the Gazza Ladra. Ninetta, Madame Sedlacech (what a name), a fine mezzo sopran and good actress. Pippo, a clumsy contra alto with good voice, but indifferent ear and execution. Gianetto, il Sig. Mazza, a disagreeable, very high tenor, almost a soprano, stiff and laborious in execution. 'Tis a difficult and unpleasing part. Ninetta's father, il Signor Benedetti, a fine bass with good style, and execution, and action. Pretty

Ballet, il Flauto Magico, (which instrument the hero played through the wrong end,) some good dancing, and charming figurante.

May 15.—In the morning we drove to Pompeia, and were much delighted with the recent discoveries in that ever-interesting illustration of ancient manners. Since I was last here in 1820, a vast deal has been discovered; among the most interesting objects, are the hot and cold baths, with their beautiful arabesques and bas reliefs; a marble bath with its inscription, and the price that it cost the donor, sixty serstices. Bathing-rooms full of remarkable arabesques; among the rest a Rape of Ganymede, and a kind of allegorical group of women and hippogriffs. Stoves and baths all very perfect. A bronze sofa, two bronze forms, niches for the urns containing unguents, supported by monsters in red stone.

In the other houses we found landscapes, temples, houses, islands, figures, &c. &c. Some good Venuses and Amphitrites, deserted Ariadnes, and Theseus stepping into his galley. But what most surprised me were two fountains in the taste of the middle ages, ornamented with cockle-shells and rough mosaic and masks; these were quite perfect, as well as the pipes and cocks which conveyed the water to them. I have seen just such fountains at Frascati and elsewhere, and know not what to think of the date of these. We saw several beautiful frescoes, principally Venuses, Ariadnes deserted by Theseus, bear-hunts, Cupids, and goats, &c. &c.; but there was one in the house of one of the fountains, resembling so nearly a *Natività*, that we all were of opinion that this house must have belonged to a Christian. Our guides told us that it was the birth of Bacchus; but I saw no similarity between the story of Semele and the painting in question, which consisted of a sitting female with an infant in her lap, a male figure in an adoring posture, two other male figures in the rear, and some goats in the foreground. There was likewise on the wall to the right hand of the fountain, an ornament or border composed of a cross of St. George and that of

St. Andrew, thus, [ornament] I never saw this ornament before. In the above-mentioned fresco was represented a plough, with its coulter and cross-bar, leaning against a wall.

Query, are these crosses and plough secret emblems of Christianity? Pompeia was destroyed in the 79th year of the Christian era; and Pliny mentions the Christians, as existing in his days, a numerous and powerful sect.

We saw several Rapes of Europa, and one of Helle, and a great deal of good landscape and figure-drawing, all in better perspective than I had imagined the ancients to have been capable of. We of course saw the theatres, amphitheatre, tombs, Sallust's villa, temples, forums, &c. &c., and returned to Naples about six o'clock, after having been stopped and *visited* by a custom-house officer at the bridge of La Maddalena. At night we went to San Carlos to see Semiramide, M°. Bonini, (good style, but *passée*); Assurro, Sig. Benedetti; Arsace, Mlle. Sedlacech: her part being for a contra alto, was therefore too low for her, as she is a soprano: all was therefore transposed and spoiled. We were all so fatigued with our day's excursion, that we fell asleep during the Ballet. Dilke left us at midnight for Rome, in company with Mr. Jerningham, Lord Stafford's son, whose acquaintance we had the pleasure of making in the steamer.

MAY 16.—I met an old acquaintance in the person of Captain Butler, D. G., who is, as well as ourselves, going to Rome. We have arranged with Sig. Angrisani to send us on in the same carriage, on Monday at daylight, by post, at fifteen Roman crowns a-head, dinner included. We are to have no trouble, the conducteur paying posts and barriers, &c. &c. We called upon the British Chargé d'Affaires and got our passports, and dined at Sir Gordon Drummond's, where we met Lord Howard of Effingham. In the evening, a number of English ladies and gentlemen came, among the rest my old friend Warren Hastings, Anderson and his spouse, Lady Belmore and Miss Caldwell, and Lady Orkney. We made some music. The

Aireys were also there, and played the guitar and sung some Spanish boleros. This morning we called upon them, and upon Admiral Taylor and his lively nieces, with whom we are to dine on Sunday.

May 17.—To-day we lionized the Studio with its matchless collection of antique bronzes, Etruscan vases, statues, &c. &c. I think that the famous group of the Farnese Bull was seen to much more advantage in the Villa Reale, than in its present place in the Statue Gallery of the Museo. The late excavations at Pompeia have added considerably to the collection of bronzes; one thing particularly attracted our notice, namely, part of a water-pipe, which had become hermetically sealed by the heat at both its ends, and contained still the water within it, which might be heard to move about. The cock of the pipe is exactly similar to those used in the great water-pipes in London and elsewhere.

The weather to-day is threatening and cooler. At three, Dalling and I dined with our friend W. H. Anderson, at the Europa. We walked in the Villa Reale in the evening, and went at half-past nine to Lady Orkney's, at the Palazzo Esterhazy. It was a dance; but I refrained from so violent an exercise in so hot an atmosphere. About eleven o'clock it rained quite hard, and we had a wet walk back again to our hotel.

MAY 18.—We decline going to the King's fête at Portici, as we are to set off to-morrow morning at daylight for Rome, and do not like the trouble of unpacking our trunks to get at our fine clothes; neither does it agree with our plans to enter much into the beau monde at this moment, lest we should regret quitting it so suddenly. All our acquaintances rally us upon our disinclination to go to Court; but we have both seen so many kings and queens that we do not care about them; and for the beauties of the Court, as we should only gaze upon them and then bid them adieu, it would tantalize us with a view of Paradise, which we could not enter. Lady Belmore wishes me to go tomorrow to dine with her and Marianna Starke among the ancients at Pompeia, but I cannot go.

This morning the weather is cool and agreeable, and the dust well laid by a copious rain all night long. *Visites de congé* occupied the morning. We dined at Admiral Taylor's, and in the evening, after walking to the Villa Reale and admiring the beau monde, went to Lady Gordon Drummond's, where we passed a pleasant hour or two; at night it rained very hard, and thundered a good deal.

MAY 19.—We set off at five o'clock, in the morning, in a voiture à quatre places, with four horses, from the Vittoria, and picked up Butler on the S$_{ta}$. Lucia. We did not leave Naples until half-past six, having another passenger to take up and much luggage. It rained hard all the morning, but the country looked green and beautiful: the mountains were all covered with clouds, so that the view was very much obscured all the day. At Gaeta we took into the carriage poor old Ponto, who was by this time quite tired of his run. We did not reach Terracina until ten o'clock at night, the heavy rain having very much cut up the roads. This inn is remarkable throughout Europe, for the badness of its accommodation and the impertinence of its people; and, in truth, I think it richly deserves its reputation. I well remember how ill we were served here eight years ago, and the astonishment of the Camareire at the jobation he received from me, who took him for the Albergatore himself. Between Naples and Terracina we counted eight several times in which our passports were demanded of us, and here our baggage was threatened with a visitation from the Doganieri; but upon paying them a few Pauls we were allowed to set off, having the trunks plombés. We left Terracina at about midnight, and passed over the marshes while we slept.

May 20.—The morning was superb, and the country looking so unlike what it was when I last travelled this road, that I could hardly believe it to be the same brown, cold, barren-looking tract which is so frequently called La bella Italia. I can now, in some degree, comprehend the ravings of poets and painters about this classic soil: Velletri, and Albano, and Gensano, embosomed in their lovely shades and woods of elm, and oak, and ilex, looked indeed like a fairy scene; and even the desert Campagna di Roma wore a coat of green and an appearance of *inhabitability* of which I had never before suspected it. In truth, one should never travel in any country during the winter, if one is in the pursuit of nature's charms. We reached the Gate of St. John Lateran at about one o'clock, and after some little delay about passports, drove to the *old Douane*, and were slightly visited by the Doganieri, who, in consideration of our professional rank and a few Pauls, would have allowed us to smuggle any thing, had we been so disposed. How little do the rulers of the earth understand how ill they are served by the minions of their inquisitorial system of custom-houses, and the agents of their ill advised schemes against the commerce of other states, and, in fact, against the true interests of their own!

I have now travelled over a great many countries, and have passed through the hands of hundreds of custom-house officers, and never yet have I seen any instance in which a little douceur would not have enabled not only myself, but my fellow-travellers, to smuggle either jewels, or books, or papers, or any thing else contraband, which could find room in the space of portmanteaus and sacs de nuits, had we felt the inclination to have so done.

We drove to the Hotel Damon, Via della Croce; and, as soon as we could change our clothes, went to the warm baths in the Via del Babuino. After dinner we strolled down to the Piazza del Popolo, to see the late improvements; I do not admire the heavy prison-looking edifices of the New Dogana and Hotel Balbi; nor do I think the two fountains and the accompanying groups of statues by any means in good taste. We mounted up the Monte Pincio, and were much pleased with the improvements which have taken place since we were all last here in 1820; we then took a turn or two in the Corso, which is the correct thing, went to the Café Ruspoli, and returned home, and went to bed at an early hour, being pretty well fatigued by our thirty-two hours' jumble in the voiture over the pavés and chaussées.

MAY 21.—We set out at half-past one to revive our recollections of the Eternal City; and first, we went to pay our devoirs to the beautiful Cenci in the Barberini Palace. What a sad story is hers, and how shamefully can what is called human justice be perverted to the worst purposes!—the expression of mild grief and placid resignation in her beautiful countenance, is something quite affecting. We walked on to the church of Santa Maria Maggiore, to St. John Lateran, and from thence to the Colosseum, which has been much repaired and restored by the present Pope; between it and the Temple of Venere e Roma, are some late excavations, which have brought to light a number of subterraneous passages, apparently the conduits for water, by which to fill the Amphitheatre during the Naumachia. The Arch of Titus has been restored in some degree, but the new work does not affect to equal the old in beauty, and is very plain, probably to prevent leading after-antiquaries astray with respect to the comparative dates. We made our bow to all the remains of the Forum, each in their turn, and ascended the Capitol to see the beautiful statue of Marcus Aurelius. The horse does indeed seem to breathe, and more than justifies Michael Angelo's emphatic address to him—" Camina."

When I compare in my mind the remains of Rome with those of Athens and Baälbeck, I am somewhat struck with their poverty and insignificance, with the exception of the Colosseum, which is indeed a wonderful mass; although I confess I cannot discover much beauty in it. There are no columns at Rome equal in size or beauty to those of Jupiter Olympius, or Minerva Parthenon, on the Acropolis, neither is there in the Eternal City so perfect a specimen as the Temple of Theseus. The Pantheon may perhaps be excepted from this observation; but it has been very much repaired and restored; while the Temple of Theseus has never been touched, and dates 2000 years ago. But Baälbeck as much outshines Athens in the size and beauty of its ruins, as Athens does Rome. After dinner we drove in the Borghese Gardens, and were pleased to observe the late improvements in the shape of a planted promenade, leading to them and an Egyptian gateway and propyleum opening into them. Indeed, Pope Leo XII. seems to be a patriotic sovereign, and to lay out a good deal of his surplus* revenue in improving this *Capital of Christendom.*

My poor old companion Ponto is very lame from his long run to Pompeia and back to Naples, and from Naples to Gaeta: he seems however to enjoy himself very much among the ruins and in the fine churches of Rome; if he lives to reach England he will indeed be a travelled dog.—I think I must write his memoirs.

MAY 22.—This morning we were occupied in

* It is a curious fact, that the Pope is at this moment the only monarch in Europe, who, without a national debt to liquidate, has a *surplus revenue.*

bargaining (or rather attempting to bargain,) with that roguish set of men the vetturini, without settling any thing decisive; after which we went to the Vatican and St. Peter's, descending into the old Basilica and inspecting all the tombs, frescoes and alto-reliefs: from hence we walked to the Palazzo Farnese, and gazed with delight upon the Galatea of the Carracci; thence to the Capitol to see the dying Gladiator and the lovely pictures of the Sibyl and St. Sebastian. We returned home pretty well tired by our walk, and I did not go out for the rest of the evening.

MAY 23.—We called at the British Vice-consul's and read the papers in his reading-room; we saw here a very beautiful specimen of Mosaic, representing, *en grand*, the Temples of Pæstum.

We made a few more attempts to arrange something with the vetturini, but all in vain, as that class of men never tell the truth. We went to see the Studios of Torwalsen, and fell desperately in love with his Venus; he is at present employed in executing a monument for

Pius VII. The figure of the venerable old Pope expresses all the sanctity of his character admirably; but I do not know what to say of the two *rectilinear*, Pagan-looking figures representing Science and Religion; the first an awkward kind of muse, and the second an Omphale clothed in the lion's skin, and treading upon the club of Hercules. There is a most lovely little Cupid feeding the doves of Venus; the expression of pleasure playing about the child's mouth, as he watches the satisfaction of his little pets, is something quite bewitching. It would be in vain for me to attempt to analyse the merits of this great man's works; his bas-reliefs, I believe, are unequalled in beauty and conception by any modern, and, I may say, by few ancient artists. The English and Danes seem to be his great patrons. I think he bids fair to surpass Canova in fame, for there is in most of his works more of poetry and less of mannerism than in those of the modern Phidias. I cannot say that I admire his group of the Graces, they are stiff and formal, and ill-grouped, and are mere mortals, and not divinities. Let me not forget to mention a splendid group of St. John preaching in the wilderness to the multitude; the attitudes of some of the listeners are quite beautiful, and more particularly that of an old man and his son, who is leaning, in a caressing manner, upon his father's shoulder. There is likewise another figure in this group which quite enchanted me; it is a little boy looking up in the face of the Man of God, with an expression of love, veneration, and attention, which it is difficult to conceive and much more so to describe. His colossal figure of Christ did not please me; it is too stiff and rectilinear; and the face is devoid of that benignity of expression, which generally characterises the divine pictures of the Italian school; it is *lack-a-daisical*, and even unpleasing. Some of the apostles, which are meant to accompany the statue of Christ, have good heads; but I was surprised to observe, that many of them were accompanied by a heathen attribute, such as cupid and an eagle. After dinner we strolled to the Fontana di Trevi and the Monte Pincio, walked to the Corso, and took our ice and coffee at the Ruspoli.

MAY 24.—Encore des Voituriers. We have now been induced to go four times to the Orso to look at the same carriage, under various pretences, by the vetturini, each of whom has sworn by St. Antonio, that it belonged to him, that we had never seen the vehicle in question, and that it had brought either Princes, or Dukes, or English gentlemen from Florence, Bologna, or Naples. The carriage is worth about five dollars, and they have the conscience to ask ten for the hire of it to Florence. I doubt whether it would go half way. It is a kind of broken-down wheelbarrow, with a head to it, and looks as if all the cats, rats, and fowls, had made their abode in it for half a century. The example of our prodigal countrymen is always quoted to justify the attempts of the natives in their exorbitant demands. I have paid long enough for being an Englishman, and think I have now travelled enough to be *free of the Continent.* In the afternoon we went to the Borghese Palace to worship the Santa Cecilia of Domenichino, and the Deposition by Raffael; and after dinner we took our usual walk upon the Pincian Hill, the evening being delightful, and some handsome women parading about. I have seen so many fine sunsets in more picturesque scenery than this, that I don't rave at the departing tints of Phœbus upon the Monte Mario, fine as they are.

MAY 25.—We drove at eleven o'clock to the Vatican, to see the Pope pontificate at the Sistine Chapel. His Holiness was so far from us, that we could not see him very distinctly. Ponto got into the chapel, but did not come in for the benediction, as he was driven out by the Swiss guards. We spent the rest of the morning in St. Peter's and the Jesuits' Church; and after dinner went to the Borghese gardens, and lionized the frescoes and statues in the palace. On our return to the Piazza Porta del Popolo, we were surprised at the number of equipages which we found coming into the city from the Ponte Molle road. It seems this is some great fête, and that the promenade is unusually crowded. We saw many very beautiful women in their carriages. We then took our usual ice at the Ruspoli, and returned home.

May 26.—Festa di San Felippo, all the Studii, and the Vatican and Galleries are shut. I asked the camariere why the Catholics were more mindful of a Saint's day than of God's? He replied, " Eh Signore! quel santo aveva fatto dei miracoli durante la vita." The inference was, then, that God had never done any miracles, and therefore was not so considerable a personage as San Felippo. I called on the Vice-Consul, and read the newspapers while it rained hard. After dinner, I walked out with Dalling towards the Ponte Molle, and saw a great many fine women. How imperious are these high Roman damas! they seem to make up in fierté for the want of character in the men, who bow the neck beneath the yoke of the Papacy. The Monte Pincio was quite deserted, cool and beautiful as it was, and all the beauty of Rome was to be seen parading in long files of carriages in the dull and gloomy Corso. 'Tis a strange taste this of the Romans. We enjoyed our ices in the garden of the Ruspoli beneath a bright moon, and under the foliage of the orange trees; after which we went to drink tea at the Vice-Consul's, where we found a handsome Roman dame, with her septuagenarian husband, and M. Teerlinck, a Dutch artist; here we played ecarté until past midnight.

May 27.—This morning we agreed with a vetturino to take us in a good roomy carriage to Florence, by way of Perugia, for forty Roman crowns, in five days and a half. We have all the carriage to ourselves. We went in the afternoon to see some studii of Mr. Wyatt's, and were much pleased with his productions, more particularly with a group of a boy protecting a pretty little girl in a storm: she is on her knees in an attitude of terror and supplication, while he, leaning over her, throws his right arm round her shoulder, and covers her bosom with her cloak; his left hand is placed very naturally upon his forehead, to save his hat from being blown away. They are both draped *à l'antique.* There is a figure full of grief and grace, of a young shepherd looking down mournfully upon a dead lamb at his feet, and a sweet little Bacchante playing with a jolly infant Bacchus. He has been successful, too, in a pretty Venus in a sitting posture, full of modesty and love. There are many other works of merit, and which denote considerable talent and originality.

From hence we went to see M. Teerlinck's pictures, (Via Capo le Case,) one of the Lake of Nemi, and one of the Pontine Marshes, with cattle drinking, and horsemen, pleased me. His figures are spirited and well projected; his trees rather too green to look natural upon canvass: there is a transparency about his water which is quite singular.

After dinner we went to see Mr. Gibson's studio, and found at the door Madame Jerome

Napoleon and suite. I own I was disappointed in the works of this artist. His most beautiful group is Psyche borne upon the arms of the Zephyrs; the youths are rather *manierés*, but she is chaste, and beautiful, and timid. There is a Venus embracing Cupid, very pretty indeed, but the lady's mouth is rather too *meretricious to be poetical*. A sleeping figure in a sitting posture, struck us as very natural and reposing. A fine group of Mars and Cupid: Mars is too young, and might be mistaken for a Jason or a Theseus. The figure of a Nymph tying on her sandal, her face denoting, like that of the Venus de Medicis, apprehension of intrusion, is pretty and well imagined.

We now took our usual walk upon the Pincian Hill, and our ices at the Ruspoli, and returned home to pack our *sacs de nuit* for to-morrow's journey to Civita Castellana.

MAY 28.—At seven in the morning we set off, leaving Captain Butler behind, as he goes on to Ancona. The Campagna and the Appennines looked quite beautiful. At 11.30. we reached Baccano, where we breakfasted in a pretty little garden at the back of the inn. I remember to have met Prince Ladaria and his party here eight years ago. At 1. 15. we set off again, and passing through the picturesque little town of Nepi, with its old castle and aqueduct, reached Civita Castellana at 6. 30. Here, to my great grief, I lost my old companion Ponto, who ran into an inn before which some carriages were standing that impeded our way, and when he came out again he found that we had moved off round a corner, and not seeing us, followed one of the other carriages which were going to Rome. We did not miss him until some time afterwards, and even then concluded that he was somewhere in the town, and would find us out. We walked about all over the town in pursuit of him, and went out on the road towards Rome, but saw nothing of him. The vetturino forwarded a message to Nepi by another coachman who was going thither, to send the poor dog back, and we still hoped that he might be found. However, the night came, and no Ponto made his appearance. The loss of this faithful brute quite distresses me, and spoils all the pleasure of my journey. I looked with a "lack-lustre eye" upon the bridge and beautiful ravine of Civita Castellana, and could eat no supper for want of my poor old Ponto to share it with me. I got no sleep all night for thinking of the distress he would be sure to feel upon discovering his error, and the loss of his master; every dog that barked I took for him, and kept opening my window and calling to him all night long.

MAY 29.—We arose at 3. 30. Still no tidings of poor Ponto. I wrote a note to our landlord at Rome, begging of him to look after the dog, and send him on to Florence by the first conveyance. I am still not without hope that some vetturino may bring him on to-day as far as Terni, where he will find us. We left the inn (I tre Mori) at 4. 15.; the morning

was beautiful, and so was the scenery, but I was out of spirits, and had not the heart to look much at it.   *   *   *
*   *   *   *   *
*   *   *   I remembered Narni quite well, and the spot from which I sketched it in 1820, and the inn where I was caught by my party taking a lesson of *Morra* from the hostler.   *   *   *
*   *   *   *   *

We reached Terni at mid-day, and here we are to repose, and in the evening go and see the Cascade. Before we set out for the Cascade, we saw a gentleman from Rome, who knew Ponto (having lodged at Damon's while we were there): he tells us that he saw him at 9. 30. this morning, between Civita Castellana and Borghetto; that the poor brute recognized him, and ran whining by the side of his carriage, trying to leap into it; *but that he was afraid the dog was mad, because his tongue was hanging far out of his mouth*, and did not venture to take him in. This man was travelling with four post-horses, and soon left my poor unhappy dog behind him to die of despair and fatigue.

Ponto has so long " eaten of my bread, and drank of my cup, and been unto me as a friend," that I feel his loss most poignantly; and the more so, when I reflect upon what the poor brute himself must now be suffering from fatigue, anxiety, and hunger. I am not sufficiently philosophical to be insensible to his affection for me, which he has shown me upon many occasions; and I feel as if I were just bereft of a very dear friend.

We walked to the Cascade; but beautiful as the scene is, and rendered dear to me by the recollections of past days, I did not enjoy the walk and the magnificent Cascade as much as I should have done, had my dear old companion been with me. On our return we drank a glass of cool excellent wine, and ate some bread and fruit at the gardener's house, in the gardens of the Princess of Poligni, and reached our wretched inn at 8. 30., where we supped ill in company with vetturini, and servants of all nations. I wrote a note to Butler, who will be here to-morrow, about poor Ponto, in hopes that he may pick him up and take him on to Bologna with him, where I shall most likely meet him.

MAY 30.—We set off for Foligno at half-past three o'clock; the morning most beautiful, and the sunrise magnificent: what a delicious country is this of the Vale of Terni! At nine we reached Spoleto, and here we breakfasted and reposed until twelve. The present Pope is said to be a native of this place, and has ornamented it with a new gate. The situation of Spoleto, with its old castle and aqueduct, is very striking. We passed through le Vene at two, and saw the pretty little temple of Clitumnus: we arrived at Foligno about six o'clock in the evening, and visited all the churches. The cathedral is magnificent, with a Baldaquin of bronze, exactly like that in St. Peter's at Rome: there is likewise in this church a celebrated Madonna; (quella di Foligno;) she is a black-looking lady enough, and is about as ugly an idol as I have ever seen. We then walked outside the town among the gardens of vines and olives, and underneath the shade of an avenue of oaks, admiring the sunsetting upon the adjacent Apennines. We were extremely well lodged at the post, and tolerably well entertained.

May 31.—We set off at half-past three in the morning, and reached Nostra Signora D.A. at six. We visited this superb temple, and examined attentively the little church of St. Francis, which it contains beneath its lofty dome, and all the paintings and frescoes relative to the story of that arch impostor St. Francis, with his blasphemous assumption of the marks of the passion of our Lord. These two remarkable churches present a good epitome of the history of this celebrated set of men, (the Franciscans) from the poverty and insignificance of their commencement, portrayed in a lively manner by their original church, up to the present day of their power and influence, typified by the soaring cupola, which covers, as it were with a shield, its diminutive parent. At half-past nine we arrived at Perugia, and here we visited the Exchange, painted by the renowned restorer of the fine arts, Pietro Vannucci (il Perugino), the lofty and beautiful cathedral, with its descent from the cross by Barrocci, (woolly and devoid of energy); a copy of Perugino's marriage of the Virgin, by a French artist, and a Madonna by Luc Signorelli; the church of the Dominicans, where there is a Madonna by Perugino; that of the Sant' Uffizio, where there is a fine painted window; and that of the Benedictines*, which is very rich in paintings by Perugino, Raphael, Albano, and Vassari. The choir is a masterpiece of the art of carving, after the designs of Raphael, and the Maître Autel is rich in precious marbles and

* This church is a fac-simile of that of Santa Maria Maggiore at Rome, and like it, has its nave supported by two rows of ancient columns. *La grande nation et ses braves*, appear to have pretty well pillaged and ransacked this strong hold of the rich Benedictines, but the treaty of Paris has restored to their owners the precious works of art which once adorned the Louvre.

pietre dure. From a balcony in the east front of this church, one has a most superb view of the lovely Valley of Perugia, with its range of Apennines and the Monte delle Sibylle, which has at this season a good deal of snow on its lofty summit.

The city of Perugia is poor and miserable; it is inundated with priests, and monks, and friars, and nuns of all colours and orders. I regretted to learn, that in the prisons of the Holy Office there are several individuals, and that the power of this odious and dreadful tribunal is still exercised in all its ancient mystery and cruelty. Nevertheless, it would seem that the morals of the regular and secular clergy are very much corrupted; but as they wield the power of the church, it hurts not them, but the luckless laic, who, no doubt, often pays the forfeit of the faults or vices of his spiritual superiors, who may transgress in secrecy and security, no man daring to question the propriety of their conduct.

We quitted Perugia at 12. 30., and reached the beautiful Lake of Thrasimene at about five halting at 6. 30. at Case del Piano. We walked out in search of il Sanguinetto, the scene of Hannibal's victory over Flaminius; but could find no traces of that battle, the ground being all covered with high and luxuriant corn. We had a fine view of the Monte Pulciano and the Apennines towards Sienna and Radicofani. We walked down towards the margin of the Lake, and returned to the miserable inn about 7. 30. to supper and bed.

JUNE 1.—At 3. 45. we left our *mosquitoed* couches, and reached Cammuccia, with its Tuscan custom-house, at 6. 30. Here we went through the form of sealing up our baggage, and for a few Pauls got a certificate of our having been *visited* (which of course was not the case).

At nine we arrived at Castiglione, and here we breakfasted extremely well, and reposed until twelve, when we set off again for Ramaggio, a few miles beyond Arrezzo, which city we passed through at five o'clock, reaching Ramaggio at 6. 30. in the evening. This is a pretty spot, upon the top of a high hill, amid forests of oak. Our host was a jolly, fat old fellow, with a numerous family, five of which were young ladies; he told me that he had *fourteen children* in *fifteen years of matrimony*. His wife, he said, was una Donna secca, secchissima (well she might be). We got nothing for supper but pigeons and sallad.

June 2.—We set off for Florence at 4, breakfasting at L'Incisa, and halting until twelve. We reached Florence at 3. 15. The customhouse officers made a show of examining our *sacs de nuit*, under the pretence of their not having been sealed up at Cammuccia. I knew what they wanted, but told them that I would not suffer them so to do, as we had a certificate from Cammuccia, and that it was not customary to visit *sacs de nuit;* that I knew full well that all they wanted was a few Pauls, which they should not have. Upon this they affected to talk big; but seeing that we made no preparations for giving up our keys, they said they concluded all was right, and let us go on.

We drove to the Albergo di Londra, nella Vigna nuova, and were indifferently lodged *au second*. We took a warm bath, and dined at six; after which we walked upon the Lungo l'Arno until dark, and went to the reading-room, in the Piazza Trinita.

JUNE 3.—After breakfast we went to the Gallery, and revisited with delight all its treasures, and the wonders of the Tribune. While here, we met our friend Mr. Ross, who had come from Malta with us, and had gone from Naples to Leghorn in the steamer. We dined at two, and called afterwards upon Lord Albert Conyngham, who is now Chargé d'Affaires *ad interim*, while Lord Burghersh is at Modena. We then went and looked at some carriages which are for sale, and talked of buying a very good strong Brussels caleche for thirty guineas. At 5. 30. we called for Mr. Ross at Schneiderf's, and drove to the Cascine, enjoying much the cool shades of that delicious promenade. Here I met Major Temple and one of his sisters, old friends of mine.

Out of a hundred people whom we might have seen at the Cascine, ninety at least were English. At nightfall there were a great many thunder-clouds, and much forked lightning towards the Vallombrosa. It is most oppressively hot; but I fear it won't rain at Florence, although it will, apparently, in the mountains.

JUNE 4.—I arose at six, and went with Dalling on foot to the Cascine to breakfast at the Café, and to sketch afterwards. I sat down in the same spot from which I made the same sketch in 1820. The Arno is much discoloured and very muddy; it must have rained hard last night in the mountains, although not a drop has fallen in the city to cool the parching atmosphere.

In the evening we went to the Palazzo Guicciardini, to call upon the Hope Johnstones, where we passed two or three hours.

JUNE 5.—Fête of Corpus Domini. Captain Boyes, an old and intimate friend of Dalling's, came and spent the whole morning with us.

We dined at Mr. Grant's, (the great Leghorn merchant,) and walked in the Cascine. We spent the evening upon the lungo l'Arno. Ross went to Rome.

June 6.—We went to the Pitti Palace, and were much pleased with that fine collection of paintings. Boyes dined with us, and went to the Cascine with us in the evening. He talks of taking a place in our carriage and accompanying us to Vienna.

June 7.—In the morning I was employed in writing letters. In the evening the Cascine and the Marchese Corsi's societé, after which we went to Captain Losack, at the Palazzo Guicciardini, where we heard some delicious singing by the Misses de Courcey. At two, we returned home, and there, to my great delight, I found my dear old Ponto, who had just been brought on here from Rome, by an English gentleman. The poor beast was so tired, and starved and weak, that he could only show his joy upon again finding his master, by whining and licking his hands and face. He will be better to-morrow after a little rest and food. I don't yet know all his adventures since he lost me at Civita Castellana; but no doubt they will add much to the interest of his history.

June 8.—This morning I went to call upon the Englishman who had brought my dog to me from Rome, and to learn from him all the particulars of the poor animal's history. It would seem that on the night of the day when we left Civita Castellana, the dog, after having sought us upon the road towards Terni, had returned to Rome in despair. He went straight, as I had anticipated, to Damon's Hotel, Via della Croce, and made such a whining and scratching at the door of the house, that M. Damon (who, it seems, had received my note from Civita Castellana that evening,) heard him; and divining what was the matter, caused the door to be opened. The poor animal staggered up stairs, to the rooms we had occupied, and would not rest until he was let in there; but to his sorrow, he did not find us. He refused all food, and never ceased his piteous moanings during the four days that he remained there. He went one day to the Custom-House in search of us, thinking, perhaps, that we might be there with our baggage, and the Douaniers; here he was seen, and followed by a Frenchman, who dodged him to Damon's, and then claimed him as belonging to himself. The waiters, however, knew better, and would not allow him to take the dog away. M. Damon gave him in charge of a voiturier, (according to my directions,) who was conducting two English gentlemen to Florence, who were lodging at his house; they having heard the history of poor Ponto, took the liveliest interest in him, and gave him room in their carriage, and had the kindness to look after him. They describe him as refusing all sustenance, and as perfectly miserable; he made no attempt to escape from them, but, on the contrary, seemed to be aware that they were his friends, and attached himself much to them, sleeping constantly in their room, and watching carefully over their effects, allowing nobody to come near them without growling and showing his jealousy of intrusion. They say, that much as they have heard and seen of the affection of dogs to their masters, they never yet knew of an instance in which the attachment of these valuable brutes was shown in so lively and affecting a manner as in this one. The dog seems to be quite sensible of the kind office they have rendered him, and has been twice this morning, ill and weak as he is, upstairs to their room to fawn upon them, and to show his gratitude.

This morning we went to see an *assaut d'armes à l'ecu de France*. Some of the fencers were good performers, but the best was young Louis Napoleon, who in the giro beat all his opponents but one, a certain Marchese, who had lately married the *sister of Lady W********. We dined at Hope Johnstone's, and met there the Losacks. In the evening, as usual, we walked in the Cascine.

JUNE 9.— We dined at Sir Grenville Temple's, at the Palazzo Mattonaja. Here we met Col.

D'Este, Prince Buttera, whom I had known at Vienna, Mr. and the Misses Baring. After dinner, we smoked *à la Turque*, in Temple's kiosk, and went to Mr. Medwin's, where we met the Visconti and several other ladies.

JUNE 10.—We paid Grazzini thirty pounds sterling for the caleche, and sixty-six Pauls for extras, having made an abatement of nearly thirty per cent. in his charges. In the evening, after our usual promenade in the Cascine, we went to the Hope Johnstones, where we met Mrs. Storey, and her two extremely pretty daughters.

JUNE 11.—To-day we dine with the Losacks, to-morrow with the Marchese Corsi, and on Friday, (Dio volente) we set off for Bologna. Dalling and Johnstone went to breakfast at the Café, in the Cascine. Old Ponto is beginning to recover his strength and spirits; he went last evening with us to the Cascine, and I am afraid, hunted and frightened a few hares and pheasants. He is still a little lame and very thin, but I think he will be able to trot along with us to Bologna, on Friday next. I spent the morning at the Gallery and the Baths at the Antichi Termi, in the Borgo S. S. Apostoli. We had a pleasant dinner party at Losack's, and a drive in the Cascine.

JUNE 12.— I walked by myself to the church of La Santa Croce, to look at the monuments of Machiavelli, Gallileo, and Alfieri. We dined at the Marchese Corsi's, where we were well entertained. In the evening we drove with the Johnstones in the Cascine, and drank our tea with them, returning home early to prepare for the morning's journey to Bologna.

CHAPTER VI.

Departure for and arrival at Bologna.—I am attacked by the fever, while at the Gallery of Pictures.—Ferrara.—Padua.—Banks of the Brenta.—Fusina.—Venice.—Piazza San Marco.—Ducal Palace.—Bridge of Sighs.—Pozzi.—Church of Saint Marc.—Arsenal.—Marchese Paulucci. - Kremnitz copper.—Reflections on the state of Venice.—Churches.—Pictures.—Canova's tomb, &c. &c.—Promenade *en bateau* to the Lido.—Departure for Trieste by steam-packet.—Trieste.—Adelsberg; its grotto of stalactites.—Conduct of inn-keeper and post-master.—Laybach.—Franz.—Mahrbourg.—Gratz.—The Semmering.—Neukirchen.—Arrival at Vienna.—Conclusion.

JUNE 13.—We set off with three posters for Bologna, at half-past five; the drive over the Apennines was most beautiful. Summer makes a wonderful difference in scenery. We reached Bologna in fourteen hours, and drove to the Pelegrino, where we were well lodged and fed.—It is a most beautifully clean hotel, with Rafaelesque ceilings and Scagliola floors. Ponto ran all the way by the side of the carriage.

June 14.—This morning I arose feverish and unwell, having had no sleep all night, for the perpetual shouting of ostlers and camarieri. After breakfast we went to the Gallery, but I was too ill to enjoy its beauties. On my way home I was seized with a vomiting-fit in the streets, accompanied by bleeding at the nose: I fear the Bolognese thought I was drunk. 'Tis a return of my Syrian fever. When I arrived at the inn I went to bed, and remained for several hours a prey to the hot fit of the fever, which did not quit me until nightfall. Dalling and Boyes nursed and attended me with the greatest kindness and assiduity, and were so good as to procure some sulphate of quinine, and to administer the necessary aperient medicines. During the night I was somewhat relieved by sleep and profuse perspiration.

June 15.—Seidlitz powders and starvation. The fever is abated, but my hands are still hot, and my tongue is foul and feverish. Ponto, as if by sympathy, is unwell also. This return of the enemy obliges me to relinquish reluctantly my project of visiting the lakes, and forces me to cut across as quickly as possible to Venice, there to repose awhile, and then get over the Alps before the excessive heats of autumn shall set in. In the evening we pushed on as far as Ferrara, through a low marshy country full of hemp and rice, corn and vines. I suffered much from violent head-ache.

JUNE 16.—The fever seized me at four in the morning while in bed. Vomiting and perspiring; cathartics and emetics filled up this miserable day. [Inn, the three crowns.]

JUNE 17.—I am better. We set out at 5. 30. for Padua, crossing the Po and the Adige. We dined at Padua, (Stella d'oro,) and set off for Venice at 5. 30: in the evening. We reached the beautiful banks of the Brenta before sunset. Here are many pretty villas, ornamented with *cockney-looking statuary.* We arrived at Fusina at 8. 15. left our carriage *en depôt* at the postmaster's, and stepped into a post gondola, reaching Venice at 9. 30.; Hotel de l'Europe. I was too much fatigued to make many observations upon this Ocean Queen.

June 18.—Thank God! I have this morning broken the chain of the fever, which has, however, left me low and debilitated enough, and totally bereft of voice. I staid at home all the morning, enjoying the view from our windows of the church of the *Salute*, and of the gondolas plying about in all directions: on my extreme left is the public garden, and the church above mentioned forms my right wing; in my front is an island, having thereon two handsome churches, and apparently an arsenal,* or depôt of some sort. After dinner we went in our gondola† down the stream, passing by the Viceregal Palace, and the beautiful Piazzetta San Marco, with its Palladian and Saracenic architecture, its columns, winged lion, Ducal Palace, and Bridge of Sighs and Prison. It is a melancholy lesson which is conveyed by this mysterious connection between human grandeur and misery. One cannot look upon these buildings without a kind of chilly thrilling of the soul.

* Il Porto Franco.
† Our gondola, with one gondoliere, cost us four francs per diem.

We now returned back again to the Grand Canal, and admired the fine palaces, and the bridge of the Rialto, familiarized as it is to our imaginations by the paintings of Cannaletto, and still more so by the immortal Shylock; we then cut through some of the back canals, among dirt, and misery, and Jews, to the Piazza San Marco, where we disembarked. I was much struck by the Oriental magnificence and beauty of its inimitable church, but disappointed in its famous horses; but I must not attempt to criticize them. We met Butler in the Piazza, but I did not venture to remain long here, fearing the night air. I must return again to this unique spot, and enjoy more at my leisure the contemplation of its beauties, and the recollection of its past glories, alas, how fallen; but still this Bridge of Sighs, this Prison, and the cruelties therein inflicted upon the victims to Patrician vengeance, serve to reconcile me to the downfal of Venice, which, however wonderful and powerful a republic, was nothing but a pure and unmixed tyranny of the privileged over the unprivileged classes.

June 19.—This day we went to the Arsenal in the gondola, accompanied by Mr. Money, the Consul, to see a ship-launch, which operation was succesfully performed. The Arsenal* is well arranged, and rather more extensive than I had imagined possible. It is three miles in circumference. There is one line-of-battle ship on the slip, " il Veneto." The model-room is pretty, and contains several neat models; among the rest are those of the *Buccentaur*, the Cæsar, of eighty guns, built by the French, some flood-gates, cranes, shears, &c. &c. We dined at the Consul's, and passed the evening at the Garden on the extreme point of land towards the Lido. Here we saw a few of the Beltà. On our return homewards, we lounged upon the Piazza San Marco, listening to a fine full Hungarian band, and looking at the Marionettes.

June 20.—Admiral Marchese Paulucci

* At its gates stand the two lions removed by the victorious Republic from the Piræus.

(Commandant-General of Marine,) called upon us to see Dalling, who had known him in the Levant, while the Marchese commanded the Imperial squadron in those seas. He told us a very remarkable fact, about the corrosion of Hungarian copper upon ships' bottoms by the salt water. He promises to send us a specimen, and a note respecting it, which we think of forwarding to the Royal Society. This copper comes from the celebrated mines of Kremnitz, in Hungary, and is the matrix of a great deal of gold and silver. It is by the process of fusion, and smelting, and separation, deprived of its more noble parts, and thus becomes very soft and malleable; and perhaps, is by this process rendered peculiarly sensible of the corrosive action of salt or of acids. I can in no other way account for the circumstance of its being so corroded and perforated.

The Italian copper from the mines near Treviso is harder, and is not liable to corrosion more than usual; but its specific gravity is not so great, neither is it so ductile as that of

Kremnitz. I have heard in our dock-yards that the oftener copper from ships' bottoms is recast, the more liable to corrosion it becomes; by a parity of reasoning, then, the corrosion of the Kremnitz copper may be accounted for. Probably also there is a greater deposit of salt in the lagoons of Venice than in most other places, from their shallowness, and the great evaporation caused by the sun's rays upon the mud at low water.

Paulucci informed us, that out of a population consisting of one hundred and twenty thousand souls, there were in Venice no less than forty thousand who were inscribed in the great book as proper objects of charity, and that these unfortunate people were actually in the habit of receiving daily a small pittance from the Government to enable them to exist! This is a frightful picture of distress, and shows how this once flourishing republic has fallen from an unprecedented height of glory and prosperity, into the very depths of calamity and humiliation.

But since the Lion of St. Mark quailed and retreated before the splendour of the Crescent; since the treasures of the East were no longer poured in prodigal abundance into the lap of the spouse of the Adriatic; since the discovery by Vasco di Gama of the passage round the southern Cape of Africa to India; and again, since the birth of a rival in the Port of Trieste, it was no longer in the nature of things that Venice should continue to be the entrepôt of the commerce of the world. The arts and the arms of her sons had indeed triumphed over almost incredible obstacles; and the boasted freedom of her political institutions had attracted to her isles the brave and the unquiet spirits of Italy, who fled hither to find an asylum against tyranny. But even Venice at last degenerated from herself; she who was once the protectress of the free and the virtuous, became the vindictive and unforgiving enemy of public virtue; she became corrupt and luxurious, cowardly and contemptible; and fell unregretted and unmourned, a dreadful lesson to surviving states.

Nevertheless, I will hope for some return of prosperity to this City of the Isles. We are credibly informed, that it is the intention of the Austrian Government to throw open the commerce of the Po, and to make Venice a free port; already an increase of commercial activity is perceptible, and the several steam-packets from Trieste and Ancona, and a new one designed to navigate the Po, cannot fail, sooner or later, to impart considerable vigour to a reviving trade and intercourse with the neighbouring provinces.

To-day I went with Boyes to see the Ducal Palace, but was sent back on account of Ponto being with me. I lionized the church of San Marco, and passed the evening at the Garden, and in the Piazza San Marco.

JUNE 21.—We went again to the Arsenal, with an order from Paulucci, and conducted thither a party of English ladies and gentlemen, viz. Colonel Cheney (of the Scotch Greys,) and family, Mrs. and Misses and Mr. Simpson and Miss Eyre. We saw the copper alluded to by Paulucci, which is corroded in a most remarkable manner. We visited the rope manufactory, the model-room, the boat-houses, blacksmiths' shops, and the ancient armoury, wherein are some very beautiful specimens of ancient armour, offensive and defensive; the helmet of Attila (*soi-disant*); a monument to Doge Emo, by Canova, beautiful and chaste; and a great many Turkish trophies, horse-tails, banners, yatagans, handjars, &c. &c.

We visited, on our return homewards, L'Academia delle belle Arti, and were much pleased with the school of statuary. Titian and Tintoretto have immortalized this collection of paintings. I did not, however, admire so much as I ought to have done, the Assumption of the Virgin by the former. His personification of the Deity is grotesque and ill contrived, and the Virgin seems tottering upon her cloud in her cumbrous robes of crimson and blue. There is likewise a little cherub, whose extended toe seems to feel for the forehead of one of the saints below, to rest upon. *But how do I dare to criticise perfection?* We saw in an adjoining room what was much more interesting than all the rest, namely, a little urn of porphyry, containing the right hand of Canova, with a simple inscription underneath it in letters of gold.

We dined to-day with the Cheneys at the Lione Bianco, and accompanied them *en gondole* upon the Laguni, and then to the Piazza San Marco, to enjoy the moonlight view and eat ices.

JUNE 22.—This morning Dalling, Boyes, and Butler, went to dine with the Marchese Paulucci on *terra firma*, leaving me to lionize the churches of Salute, Redemptore, San Giorgio, &c. &c. the Ducal Palace, with its pictures, statues, dungeons,* and Bridge of Sighs; from thence to the Rialto, and then some ice in the Piazza, returning home tired and

* I shall not attempt to describe these dreadful Pozzi, or the sensations they awoke in my bosom; the topic is too harrowing to dilate upon; and again, these scenes of misery have been too ably described to need any observation from me.

heated, to dress for dinner with the Cheneys at three.

In the evening all the ladies and ourselves of the male sex went in three gondolas to the Lido, and walked upon the shores of the Adriatic, returning to the boats at the Jews' burying-ground, and thence home, enjoying as we went a fine storm of thunder and lightning, which hung over, and seemed to menace the city of St. Mark with destruction. The Piazza San Marco, and ices, and Marionettes terminated the day.

JUNE 23.—This day we lionized the pictures at the Palazzo Manfrini, the churches of Santa Maria dei Frati* and San Roque, and the celebrated Paulo Veronese at the Palazzo Pisani. After dinner we went to the Garden and the Piazza San Marco, where we staid until a late hour.

* In this church is the tomb of Canova, raised over his remains by the most celebrated of his pupils. It is an imitation, and in some degree a copy, of his famous work in the church of the Augustins in Vienna. Here is likewise a flat stone on the pavement, indicating the place where Titian reposes.—Oh, blush, Venetians!

June 24.—To-day the church of San Giovanni e Paulo.* Dinner at the Lione Bianco. Promenade, *en bateau*, to the Vice-regal Palace. Thunder, lightning, and rain. We returned to the Lione Bianco, and passed the evening very agreeably with music.

June 25.—After making *mes visites de congé*, I mounted with Dalling to the top of the Tower of St. Mark, from whence is perhaps one of the finest bird's-eye views in the world. I am not quite sure whether it does not surpass that from the top of the Tower of Galata. Nobody leaves Venice without making the purchase of a few necklaces, chains, &c. &c. and I furnished myself with some, as *petits cadeaux*, for my fair friends at Vienna and in England.

At nine in the evening, we embarked on board of the steam-packet for Trieste, where we found our caleche, which the agent for

---

* In this handsome church is a picture by Titian, called, I know not why, the Martyr St. Peter. I don't admire it.— It is not near so fine as that by Domenichino, of the same subject (or something very like it,) at Bologna.

packets had sent for to Fusina. The weather was threatening and dark; but, luckily for me, the water was quite smooth, so that I was not sea-sick.

JUNE 26.—We reached Trieste at half-past six in the morning. The view of this fine city, seated at the foot of lofty mountains, its ports and quays crowded with shipping, is cheerful and imposing.

After disembarking all our gear, we walked to two or three hotels in search of accommodation; but finding nothing to suit us, we resolved upon pushing on towards Vienna, which, after reconnoitring the city, its quays, canals, bridges, squares, churches, &c. &c. we did, with three post-horses, at half-past ten.

Upon leaving Trieste, we came to an enormously steep hill, and here we put on two extra horses. From the summit of the mountain is a prodigiously fine view of the Adriatic, of the Friouli Alps, of the coasts of Istria and Lombardy, and of Trieste at your feet.

We soon came to the Douane, and here we

were gently visited by the German functionaries, who were exceedingly civil, and apparently much pleased at being spoken to in their own language.

We reached Adelsberg at half-past six, and went to visit its famous cavern of stalactites. This great natural curiosity amply repays the traveller, who may have come a thousand miles to see it. It is situated on the side of a steep hill, looking down upon a tranquil little valley full of pasture and cattle. It contains in its bosom an assemblage of the most extraordinary phenomena; such as lagoons, rivers, waterfalls, galleries, bridges, staircases, thrones, pulpits, cathedrals, statues of men and beasts, groves of trees, floods of diamonds, and, in short, every astonishing variety of stalactical formation which it is possible for the most vivid fancy to conceive. This wonderful cavern extends for many miles into the bowels of the mountain, and our guides assured us that they had wandered on for two or three days together, without finding any termination of its labyrinths.

They mentioned that the skeleton of a man, perfectly petrified, had been found here; but I am not quite convinced that they might not have mistaken some one of the natural incrustations of the cavern for the miserable object alluded to.

Reichard, however, mentions, that in 1818, in a grotto near Adelsberg, the stalactite of the skeleton of a man was found, with that of an antediluvian animal, which is now to be seen in the Museum at Trieste.

The effect produced by the glare of torches, and the echoes of our footsteps and voices in these subterranean regions, was something quite supernatural. I did not venture to remain above an hour and a half here, fearing an attack from my agueish enemy.

We returned to the inn at half-past eight; and after supping pretty well at the table d'hôte, retired to our repose at ten.

JUNE 27.—It rained heavily in the morning. We found our bill at the inn exorbitant, and resisted paying it; but in vain! The sturdy landlord, a bullying sort of courier-looking fellow, who had served in the French armies, and therefore looked upon himself as a gentleman, refused to abate a single iota of his charge. In vain we offered what we considered an ample remuneration; in vain we ordered the postilions to proceed; they were inflexible, and apparently in league with the landlord.

We went to the Post-office, and knocked up the postmaster; we appealed to his pride, and asked him if it were consistent with his dignity, as a public officer of the Emperor's, to allow his servants to be deterred from doing their duty by the menaces or influence of an innkeeper, and if it were lawful to detain travellers at the beck of a cheating and insolent keeper of a tavern. His German apathy could not resist the force of our arguments; and after looking at the bill, and agreeing with us that it was grossly exorbitant, he accompanied us to the inn, and ordered the postilions to proceed. They jumped into the saddles, and were setting off, when out sallied the terrible innkeeper, backed by his wife, daughter, chamber-maids, and waiters, and opposed our departure. The postmaster was intimidated, and sneaked off, recommending us to suffer ourselves to be cheated, and depart, rather than delay ourselves by a long and tedious appeal to the police, in the which we should lose both time and money, and, after all, obtain no justice.

Bestowing a few agreeable epithets upon *M. l'aubergiste militaire*, we paid the money, and set off at half-past seven for Laybach.

Laybach is a beautifully situated and deliciously clean and agreeable city. Here I felt that I had returned to Germany, and as if I had come back to my native land, or to one which I loved as well. The sound of the German language awakened a thousand emotions in my bosom; and the consciousness of approaching dear Vienna, and the hope of seeing once more all my friends in that delightful city, quite inspired me.

There is a loyalty and *bonhommie* about the German nations which certainly constitute a great charm. They are, it is true, slow and methodical; but they are good, frank, industrious, and sober people; and as for beauty, I must say, that I know no country where it is more abundant, and more particularly among that class of females who wait at table in all the inns in the South of Germany, [die Kellnerinnen,] whose fascinating style of dress, and coquetish and graceful manners, are the most attractive things possible.

Apropos des Kellnerinnen. We were waited upon at the excellent inn at Laybach (the post) by two lovely creatures of this class.

Laybach is situated upon the river Sau; it is celebrated for its agreeable promenades of Auersperg and Eggenberg, for its handsome churches, public buildings, plays, masked balls, library, cabinet of natural history, &c. &c., and, above all, for its having been the seat of the Congress of 1821.

We reached Franz at nightfall, and were well lodged at the post, situated in a lovely valley; and here, as at Laybach, we were attended by three most beautiful Kellnerinns.

It rained furiously all the night long.

JUNE 28.—The rain continued all the morning, so we remained snugly in bed until eight o'clock, setting off at nine for Mahrbourg.

Our journey of to-day lay through a lovely country, in which the population appeared to be happy and thriving. Mahrbourg is a large straggling town, situated upon the river Drau : it is in Styria, and, with the exception of Gratz, is the most populous town in that province.

We were tolerably lodged at the post.

JUNE 29.—The morning was deliciously fine; and the country, especially as we approached Gratz, was enchanting. Gratz is the capital of Styria, and is a large, well-built, handsome, and cleanly city. We reached it at half-past twelve, and drove to the post, where we were extremely well lodged and entertained, dining in the restaurant. The Kellnerinns were bewitching.

In the evening we lounged to the " Lust Garten," where we devoured ices and fruit, &c. and walked round the beautiful glacis, the favourite promenade of the fair Grätzerinnen, and here we saw many lovely forms and faces.

Gratz is one of the most tempting-looking cities which I have ever visited; it is renowned for the agreeable nature of its society, for its promenades, public gardens, baths, plays, balls, &c. &c. The fair sex has been in all times celebrated for its beauty. [See *Reichard.*] It contains many churches, squares, palaces, and other objects worthy of attention. It has manufactories of silk stuffs, steel, and iron, and plenty of breweries of excellent beer. It has likewise the additional *agrément* of being in the centre of a wine country. Its population is thirty thousand.

Some year or two ago, I thought of establishing myself here for a time, and have, indeed, at this moment, in my possession letters of introduction to some of the principal people here, from my kind friend Count Sauerow; but as I could not tarry long here at present, I did not think of presenting myself *chez ces aimables personnes.*

June 30.—We set off for Bruck at five in the morning. The view of Gratz, as we looked back upon it from a little distance, was quite enchanting.

We dined at Bruck about one o'clock. This pretty little town I well remembered, having been here in the autumn of 1826. Here we took leave of the river Muhr, by which we had driven all the day.

Between Maerzuschlag and Schottwein we saw a most superb and remarkable rainbow, with an image of itself reflected above it; this second arc being quite perfect, and nearly as brilliant as its parent. The rainbow seemed to support upon itself all the weight of the black and threatening looking atmosphere above it, while all below it was quite clear and serene, the trees and vegetation being completely coloured by the various tints of the prism, which poured out floods of glory from the extremities of the arch, as it spanned the deep ravine, and rested upon either side of the valley.

Before we reached Schottwein, we came to a

high hill, upon the summit of which is a handsome marble monument, which marks the limits of Styria. This hill is called the Semmering; from hence is a fine view of the Snaeberg.

The valley of the Muhr is beautiful; it is full of fine houses, and the summits of its hills on either hand are crowned with romantic-looking old castles.

The descent from the Semmering is very remarkable; the defile being by nature extremely strong, and reinforced by walls and towers of ancient date.

We reached Neukirchen at eleven, and found every body in bed. Here our accommodation was very bad; and I was very much amused by the amazement and *embarras* of my companions upon beholding the huge *duvets* and lack of sheets, which characterise the beds of a German country inn.

July 1.—We set off for Vienna at six o'clock. The weather was delightfully fine and cool; and the plains of Austria, bounded by the

Hungarian hills and Styrian mountains, looked beautiful and fertile.

As we approached Vienna, we met Madame de Laykam, (Prince Metternich's mother-in-law). I stopped the carriage, and jumped out to speak to her. My Greek cap and late illness had so much altered me, that she did not at first recognise me. She was on her way to Waltersdorff, to see the Prince and Princess, who were residing there for the summer.

As we passed by Baāden and Mödling, and all those charming spots, my heart beat with pleasurable and painful emotions at the same time; for here I had passed a summer under circumstances which, although I cannot think of them without pain, were wound up with so many real pleasures, and so many of those tender and interesting enjoyments, which form the principal charm of our existence, and the greatest alleviation of the sorrows incident to the lot of humanity, that I cannot recall them at this moment without an indescribable sensation about the heart, and an irresistible suffusion of the eyes.

We reached the barrier of Vienna at half-past twelve; and were a good deal plagued by the Douaniers about some Turkish tobacco belonging to my friend Dalling, which they put under temporary, (as they said,) confiscation, and moreover obliged him to pay a deposit of twelve florins and a half upon it.

We drove to the Kaiserinn von Oësterreich in the Weybourg Gasse; so here I am in my old quarters, after an absence from Vienna of something more than *fifteen* months.

CONCLUSION.

DEAR READER,

I HAVE now brought you, as well as myself, safely back again to Vienna, after an absence of fifteen months, during which time I have passed through many interesting countries. I know not how it is, that to almost every traveller but myself, some terrible adventure happens, while to me, alas!. no fiery dragon, imprisoned damsel, enchanted castle, or spiteful wizard, would appear, although I did all I could to invoke them. In vain I hoped that something would occur to give my narrative a romantic or interesting cast; I was obliged to content myself with the sober realities of human life;

but, God be praised, I have neither been plundered by roving Arabs, bastinadoed by savage Turks, nor carbonadoed by Greek pirates; and if (as I fear you will find it) my book contains nothing that is worth the reading, and much less worth the writing, and you should very naturally ask the question why I took the trouble to compile so many stupid pages, I have no excuse to offer, other than this humble one, namely, that they were written exclusively for the amusement of my own family, and for those eyes which would perhaps glisten with pleasure as they dwelt upon the unstudied lines of the wandering pilgrim.

Be indulgent to my little book, kind reader, and remember that it naturally partakes in too many instances of the style of a journal, from the hurried manner in which it was written; the want of leisure and convenience very often preventing me from attending to the manner of my composition.

Some parts are more carefully put together than others, and these have generally been written under circumstances more favourable to the Muses.

I might easily have swelled my work into two thick Volumes, containing my Tour in Holland and Belgium, the provinces of the Rhine, Wurtemberg, Bavaria, a winter at Munich, with its court and society; the descent to Vienna upon a raft, on the Danube; my summer residence at Bäaden, in Austria, with its "*Gesellchafts bad*," or *bain de societé*, &c. &c.; my Tour in the Tyrol, Salz Kammerguts, and Styria, and a winter and carnival at Vienna, with a description of its *haute societé*; theatres, operas, promenades, manners, and customs, &c. &c. All of these I could have embellished with sketches, of which I made abundance; but I felt that many other authors had preceded me over so well-beaten a track, and that I had little or nothing new to offer; and, moreover, I dreaded the imputation of "book-making;" so that, after some consideration, I determined upon limiting my book to my Tour from Vienna to Constantinople, and my return to Austria; the latter part of which, I am well aware, must be totally devoid of interest, but was necessarily included to make the tour complete.

I have now only to add, that I remained with my *compagnons de voyage* three weeks at Vienna, showing them some of the objects most worthy of notice; revisiting all my old haunts in the environs, seeing some of my friends who remained in the neighbourhood, and more particularly my kind patron, Prince Metternich, with his then beautiful (but now, alas! departed) Princess, her parents and family.

To this eminent statesman, and most accomplished and polite gentleman, I had the pleasure of presenting, as the only tribute of gratitude for past kindnesses which I could offer him, a cone from the cedars of Mount Lebanon, which I had gathered and carefully preserved expressly for him. He accepted it in the most affectionate manner; assuring me, that no present that he had ever received gave him greater pleasure, inasmuch as it was a strong proof of regard in one who could think of him in such a place, and under such circumstances.

Indeed, the interest which was excited among all my friends, by my return to them after my rambles, was the most flattering thing possible to my *amour propre*, and I felt compensated for all that I had gone through and suffered, by witnessing it.

Nothing particular occurred to me during my stay, which was enlivened now and then by a dinner at Lord Cowley's, Prince Metternich's, M. de Tettenborn's, la Comtesse Palatine de Potocka, Mr. Bradford's, and a few other friends'; and by a great ball at Baaden, at which all the Court, except the Emperor, assisted. This fête took place during the most tremendous storm of wind, thunder, and lightning, that I ever witnessed. It was impossible to face it in the streets; tiles, chimney tops, stones, and dust, flying about in the most terrific manner, amid the awful flashes of lightning, and roars of thunder. Many carriages were completely blown over, on their return through the plains; large trees were uprooted, and the roads were strewn with branches for miles together;—in short, it was a complete hurricane.

Lord Heytesbury, with Captain A'Court, Lord Bingham, and the suite, were staying, as well as ourselves, at the "Kaiserinn von Oesterreich," awaiting their final instructions. I lent my journal through Hungary, Transylvania, Wallachia, Bulgaria, and Roumelia, to Captain A'Court, thinking that he might perhaps some day have to pass through part of those countries. They quitted Vienna before we did, and went to Odessa by a more northern route, through Leopold, in Gallicia.

I had two attacks of fever and ague during my stay.

We left Vienna, for England, in the latter end of July; and, taking the route of Prague, Töplitz, Dresden, Leipsig, Lützen, Weimar, Erfurth, Gotha, Fulda, Frankfort-upon-Mayn, and Mayence, embarked ourselves, Ponto, and the britchka, in the steam-boat, and went rapidly down the lovely Rhine, to Rotterdam; at which last city I arrived, after somewhat more than three years' absence, on the eighth of August 1828.

The rest is shortly told: another steam-boat (the Attwood, of London,) landed me, after a rapid passage of twenty-six hours, at the dirty and disagreeable Custom-house wharf, in London, on the sixteenth of August.

And now, dear reader, let me once more implore your indulgence for all my errors and all my faults; and let me intreat you to bear in mind, that mine is a mere "Personal Narrative," and that if selfish feelings and domestic allusions are too often obtruded in my pages, remember that I could not well blot them out without totally altering the character of my Journal.

Adieu,

C. C. F.

London, May, 1828.

APPENDIX.

ARABIC NUMERALS.

1. — Wahad	31. — Whad-tellateen,
2. — Tennen	&c. &c. &c.
3. — Tellati.	40. — Arbāeen
4. — Araab	41. — Whad-arbāeen,
5. — Hamsi	&c. &c. &c.
6. — Sitti	50. — Hamseen
7. — Sebāa	60. — Sitteen
8. — Temani	70. — Sebaateen
9. — Tessa	80. — Temenieen
10. — Ashra	90. — Tessateen
11. — Hadarsh	100. — Mieyieh
12. — Knarsh	101. — Muyiehoawahad
13. — Hattaash	200. — Mieten.
14. — Arbaatash	300. — Tellati-mieyieh
15. — Hamstash	1000. — Elef
16. — Sittash	2000. — Elfen
17. — Sebaatash	3000. — Tellatelef
18. — Tementash	4000. — Arbaatelef
19. — Tessatash	5000. — Hamsielef
20. — Ashreen	6000. — Sitelef
21. — Whad-ouashreen,	7000. — Sabatelef
&c. &c. &c.	8000. — Tementelef
30. — Tellateen	9000. — Tessatelef,
	&c. &c. &c.

VOCABULARY OF ARABIC.

Where's my Turban	—	When lefti
Jacket	—	Shentyen
Sash	—	Zenari
Shoes	—	Surmeti
Slippers	—	Alchini
Vest	—	Mentien
Shirt	—	Amiss
Boots	—	Djezmar
Cap	—	Ahkiey
Cloak	—	Mushlah
Watch	—	Seyati
Handkerchief	—	Mandeel
Knife	—	Zecchin
Spoon	—	Mallahāā
Fork	—	Shokey
Plate	—	Sackan
a Light	—	Dow
Trowsers	—	Shalva
Drinking Glass	—	Kübayeih
Carpet	—	Tonksey, or Sejady
Mat	—	Hassideh
Give me a Stick	—	Attini adib
some Bread	—	Schweit hobs

Give me Wine	—	Attini Enbeet
Water	—	Moy
Milk	—	Halieb
Meat	—	Lachem
Eggs	—	Beed
Oil	—	Zeitt
Salt	—	Melch
Pepper	—	Fullfull
Coffee	—	Finjan Cajuey
Grapes	—	Aneb
Figs	—	Tyn
Apricots	—	Mushmush
Sword	—	Saif
Pistols	—	Tapanjat
Musquet	—	Barroudi or Bundkieh
Powder	—	Barout
Shot	—	Hourds
Bullets	—	Ressaz
Where's my Dog?	—	When Kelby?
My Dog	—	Kelby
Dog	—	Kelb
Give my Dog to eat	—	Arti Kelby shi ta yecol
Make my bed	—	Armel Farshty
Saddle my Horse	—	Shed serge al Hssany
Horse	—	Hssan
Hold my Horse	—	Hed el Hssan
Thank you, Sir	—	Kattel Herak
Come here	—	Taal hone
Go away	—	Rhu minhone
Make haste	—	Rhu kawem
Come here, you fellow	—	Tayia Radjel
boy	—	Sabbi

Come here, you youth	—	Tāāl hone Shubb
young woman	—	Sabeieh
old ditto		Mahrah
Bring the book	—	Jib el Kitteb
Have you any Copper Coins?	—	Aān Cōon Slaheet nhass
Yes	—	Nāam, eh
No	—	La
There is	—	Fee
There is not	—	Mafee
a little	—	Fee a leel
much	—	Fee kiteer
Good morning	—	Sabah el hair
evening	} —	Messicum bil hair
night		
Good bye	—	Hattricum
God bless you	—	Māā
I'll flog you	—	Bud drubeck
I'll shoot you	—	Be ausack
Will you take a walk with me?	} —	Bittrou shim il haoua mai?
Impossible	—	Mabissir
With pleasure	—{	Kramt hartrack, or Allah rasi
How d'ye do?		
Are you well?	} —	Taibine or Keef halleck
Are they well?		
I am well, are you well?	..{	Taib, or Mabsout ham'd Allah?
Your good health	—{	Taoul a marcom-Taoul omrack, or Mahabedcom
Much good may it do you	—	Sacher, or Sachaten

APPENDIX. 307

I	—	Anna
Thou, or you	—	Enti
He	—	Whoey
She	—	Hehiey
It	—	Ill
We	—	Nehana
Ye, or you	—	Gennabeck or Hadreteck
They	—	Hinno
Purse of Piastres	—	Kiss
Dollar	—	Real franca
Silver	—	Fadda
Gold	—	Daheb
Brass	—	Nhass
Saddle	—	Serge
Bridle	—	Ladjem
Whip	—	Amsha
Stirrup	—	Ircubet
Stable	—	Staboul-yahour
House	—	Bait
Barley	—	Sheir
Straw	—	Tibben
Beans	—	Fool
Village	—	Deaā
Town	—	Medine-Bellad
Convent	—	Deir
Paper	—	Warka
Pens	—	Kallem
Ink	—	Hebr
Wafers	—	Boursham
Bring	—	Jib
Take away	—	Hoad shiloh

Satan	—	Sheitāān
Saddle bags	—	Hurge
Paras	—	Musrieh, riet
Two Piastres	—	Ursh-en
A Tree	—	Sejar
The	—	El'
Plague	—	Stahoun

APPENDIX.

TABLE OF POSTS.

Date.	Names of Towns.	No. of Posts.	Hour of arrival.		Expense of horses.		Expense of postil.		Remarks.
			H.	M.	flor.	kr.	flor.	kr.	
March 24.	From Vienna to Schwegat	1	11	0 A.M.	2	24	1	20	
	Fishament	1	0	15 P.M.	1	36	1	0	
	Riegelsbrunn	1	1	20	1	36	1	0	
	Hoemburg	1	3	40	1	36	0	57	
	Kittsee	1	5	0	1	36	1	0	
	Ragendorff	1	7	0	1	36	1	0	
	Wieselborg	1	10	0	1	20	0	40	
25.	Hochstrass	1½	1	50 A.M.	2	0	1	12	
	Raab	1	3	55	1	20	0	40	Here we entered Hungary.
	Göngo	1	6	15	1	20	0	40	Three horses.
	Aaes	1	8	20	1	20	0	40	
	Cormon	1	9	50	1	20	0	42	
	Nesmühl	1¼	0	40 P.M.	1	40	0	50	
	Neudorf	1	3	55	2	0	0	45	
	Derogh	1	6	0	2	0	0	40	
	Vorsowar	1½	10	5	3	0	1	20	
	Ofen [Poste Royale]	1½	12	30 P.M.	3	0	1	36	
26.	Pest	left post at	8	0 A.M.					
	Soroskar	1	8	45	2	0	0	46	
	Oesa	1	9	45	2	0	0	43	
	Inaez	1	11	40	2	0	0	43	
	Oerkenny	1	2	15 P.M.	2	0	0	48	
	Foldeak	1	4	0	2	0	0	40	
	Kelskemet	1	6	0	2	0	0	56	
	Paka	1	8	20	2	0	0	40	
	Feleygehaza	1	10	40	2	0	0	40	Four horses.
27.	Petery	1	2	25 A.M.	2	40	0	50	
	Kistelleck	1	5	45	2	40	0	53	
	Sztmaez	1	8	20	2	40	0	53	
	Szegedin	1	10	10	2	40	0	50	
	Horgos	1¼	1	0 P.M.	3	20	0	50	
	Kleinkan	1	3	0	2	40	1	30	
	Mokren	1½	6	30	4	0	1	0	
	Comlos	1	9	15	2	40	0	40	
	Csadat	1	10	0	2	40	0	40	
28.	Klein Petch	1¼	1	30 A.M.	3	20	0	40	
	Temeswar	1¼	5	0	3	20	0	50	
	Rekas	2	8	15	5	20	1	0	
	Kisetto	1	10	40	2	40	0	40	
	Lugos	1	0	25 P.M.	2	40	0	40	

Date.	Names of Towns.	No. of Posts.	Hour of arrival.	Expense of horses.		Expense of postil.		Remarks.
			H. M.	flor.	kr.	flor.	kr.	
March								
28.	Boskur........	1½	5 40 P.M.	4	0	0	30	
	Fasect	1	7 25	2	40	0	40	
	Kossowar......	1	9 0	2	40	0	40	Chaussee.
	Kosset	1	12 12	2	40	1	0	
29.	Dobra	1	2 25	2	40	0	40	Six horses.
	Lessnech	1	5 40	4	0	0	50	
	Deva	1	8 45	4	0	0	50	Five horses, paid for four.
	Szaswarrow	1½	0 30	5	0	1	0	
	Siboth	1	3 0	2	40	0	40	
	Muhlenbach....	1¼	6 45	3	20	0	50	
	Reismarkt	1¼	10 40	3	20	0	50	
30.	Magh	1	3 40 A.M.	4	0	0	50	
	Hermanstadt ..	1	6 10	4	0	0	50	
	Rothenthurm ..	1½	9 40	3	0	0	40	
	Lazaretto......	1	1 15 P.M.	4	0	1	20	
	Kinnin........	1	5 0	6	0	1	20	
31.	Perikan	1½	0 35			0	30	N.B. Upon our rival at Bucharest
	Satatroick	1½	5 0			0	35	found that our ho
April	Kurté d'Argish	2	11 45			1	20	toble friend, the
1.	Munichest	1	10 5 A.M.			1	46	Master at Kinnin, surcharged us co
	Petesti	1	1 40 P.M.			0	25	derably in the po
	Korchintof	1½	5 20			0	30	money; and by the terference of M. P
	Gagest	1¾	8 35			0	35	three ducats an
	Maranches	1½	11 50			0	38	half were retunde the post-office.
2.	Florest	1½	2 50 A.M.			0	35	
	Bollentina	1	5 50			0	35	
3.	Bucharest	3	8 45			0	30	
	Vidra		3 45 P.M.					From Ruschuck
	Guastanet		5 50					the south side of Danube, unto Con
	Pietri		6 45					tinople, we had
	Tya		9 0					horses, including
4.	Giurgevo		6 30 A.M.					own two, the tar's, the postili
	Rasgratz		9 10 P.M.					and the baggage ho
	Shumla		0 0					Our bargain with Tartar was 1300
	Dragoleu		5 30					tres, but at Kirk (or Kirk Illisia) were defrauded b
5. 6.	Chali Kavack ..		11 45					Post Master, obliged us to pay ducats more, and
7.	Carnabat		1 15 A.M.					our arrival at Con tinople we made
	Faki		6 0 P.M.					Tartar a presen four ducats.
8.	Kirk Issa		4 30					whole expense o
9.	Burgaz........		4 45 A.M.					journey from Vi to the capital of Tr
	Tchorlu		8 30 P.M.					did not much ex 25l. a head.
10.	Buados........		5 45					
11.	Constantinople .		4 0					

LONDON:
PRINTED BY S. AND R. BENTLEY,
Dorset Street, Fleet Street.

14 DAY USE
RETURN TO DESK FROM WHICH BORROWED

LOAN DEPT.

This book is due on the last date stamped below,
or on the date to which renewed. Renewals only:
Tel. No. 642-3405
Renewals may be made 4 days prior to date due.
Renewed books are subject to immediate recall.

JUL 20 1972 3 0

REC'D LD AUG 1 72 -9 PM 8 0

LD21A–60m-8,'70
(N8837s10)476—A-32

General Library
University of California
Berkeley